CASEBOOK IN
ABNORMAL PSYCHOLOGY
Fifth Edition

John Vitkus
Cleveland Clinic Foundation

CASEBOOK IN ABNORMAL PSYCHOLOGY
Fifth Edition

John Vitkus
Cleveland Clinic Foundation

Boston   Burr Ridge, IL   Dubuque, IA   Madison, WI   New York   San Francisco   St. Louis
Bangkok   Bogotá   Caracas   Kuala Lumpur   Lisbon   London   Madrid   Mexico City
Milan   Montreal   New Delhi   Santiago   Seoul   Singapore   Sydney   Taipei   Toronto

Higher Education

Casebook in Abnormal Psychology, Fifth Edition

Published by McGraw-Hill, an imprint of The McGraw-Hill Companies, Inc., 1221 Avenue of the Americas, New York, NY 10020. Copyright 2004, 1999, 1996, 1993, 1988 by The McGraw-Hill Companies, Inc., All rights reserved. No part of this publication may be reproduced or distributed in any form or by any means, or stored in a data base or retrieval system, without the prior written permission of The McGraw-Hill Companies, Inc., including, but not limited to, in any network or other electronic storage or transmission, or broadcast for distance learning.

1 2 3 4 5 6 7 8 9 0   DOC/DOC   0 9 8 7 6 5 4 3

ISBN 0-07-295186-9

http://www.mhhe.com

For my patients,
who taught me with their wisdom
and inspired me with their strength.

CONTENTS

CASE 1: WORRIED SICK
Generalized Anxiety Disorder   1

CASE 2: ANXIETY RUSH
Panic Disorder   17

CASE 3: 9-11 WILL NOT BE FORGOTTEN
Post-Traumatic Stress Disorder   25

CASE 4: CLEANLINESS IS NEXT TO GODLINESS
Obsessive-Compulsive Disorder   33

CASE 5: ALTERED STATES
Dissociative Identity Disorder   41

CASE 6: BIG WOMAN ON CAMPUS
Bipolar Disorder, Manic Episode   49

CASE 7: WHO CARES ABOUT OLD CARS?
Major Depressive Disorder   59

CASE 8: NEVER GOOD ENOUGH
Dysthymia with Dependent Personality Disorder   69

CASE 9: ROAD RAGE
Intermittent Explosive Disorder   79

CASE 10: RIDING THE RELATIONSHIP ROLLERCOASTER
Borderline Personality Disorder   89

CASE 11: NEVER TOO YOUNG TO QUIT
Alcohol Dependence   103

CASE 12: SHOOTING UP
          Opioid Dependence   117

CASE 13: IS VIAGRA ENOUGH?
          Male Erectile Disorder   133

CASE 14: LOSING YOUR GRIP
          Schizophrenia, Residual Type   143

CASE 15: WHY CAN'T I SLEEP?
          Primary Insomnia   155

CASE 16: A FADING MEMORY
          Dementia of the Alzheimer's Type   165

CASE 17: DIRTY FOOD
          Bulimia Nervosa   175

CASE 18: ON THIN ICE
          Anorexia Nervosa   185

CASE 19: A QUIET FOG
          Attention-Deficit Disorder, Inattentive Type   193

CASE 20: I CAN'T LIVE WITHOUT YOU
          Separation Anxiety Disorder   201

CASE 21: LIFE AFTER MAINSTREAMING
          Moderate Mental Retardation   213

CASE 22: IN A WORLD OF HIS OWN
          Autistic Disorder   221

SELECTED REFERENCES   235

PREFACE

Casebook in Abnormal Psychology, Fifth Edition consists of 21 case histories based on my professional experience and additional material supplied by mental health professionals. The presenting symptoms were actually observed, and the therapeutic techniques were actually administered. To maintain confidentiality, information that could identify individuals has been changed. Any resemblance to real persons is coincidental.

The 21 cases survey a variety of psychiatric diagnoses that follow the conventions of the American Psychiatric Association's *Diagnostic and Statistical Manual of Mental Disorders, Fourth Edition, Text Revision*, often abbreviated as *DSM-IV-TR*. Each case is divided into four sections: Presenting Complaint, Personal Background, Conceptualization and Treatment, and Prognosis. These sections discuss, respectively, (1) the circumstances that brought the person to therapy at that time; (2) developmental, family, or other influences that may have contributed to the current problem, (3) the therapist's understanding of the case and plan of treatment; and finally (4) an estimation of the likely outcome of the therapy. In a general way, this organization reflects how mental health professionals approach their cases and communicate with each other.

Cases are presented within particular treatment approaches. **Please note:** By presenting a particular treatment with each disorder, I am *not* implying that the treatment presented is the "correct" approach for that problem. It may not be the most effective—or even the most common—treatment offered for that disorder. However, it was an actual treatment provided by an actual therapist to patients with similar symptoms.

This book was written with four primary goals. The first is to provide readers with a detailed and vivid account of the symptoms that characterize various disorders. The second is to highlight the differences in various therapeutic approaches. The third is to illustrate just how these therapeutic approaches are actually put into practice in the course of treating specific psychiatric symptoms. The fourth is to acquaint the reader with the benefits and limitations of professional intervention in everyday practice.

This edition differs from previous editions in three primary ways. First, it updates and expands upon earlier editions by incorporating the terminology of *DSM-IV-TR* and by the addition of new cases. Also, the reader should be aware that over the past 15 years the treatment of mental problems has been changed dramatically by the implementation of cost containment strategies known collectively as managed care. Some of these cases occurred before managed care was widely implemented, and as a result some of the treatments described would be seen as quite luxurious by today's more spartan standards. Finally and most noticeably, for the sake of improved readability the cases in this edition were simplified to focus specifically on the therapeutic process and less on background research. Readers are of course encouraged to probe the topics presented in this book in greater depth by consulting their textbooks, consulting with faculty and clinical staff, and through the Internet.

ACKNOWLEDGMENTS

I am very grateful to the following consultants for their time, help, and expertise. Their generosity provided me with a fascinating behind-the-scenes view of the therapeutic process.

Mark Bondeson, Psy.D.
VA Medical Center, Brecksville, OH

Ellie Bragar, Psy.D.
private practice, New York, NY

Dana Brendza, Psy.D.
Cleveland Clinic Foundation, Cleveland, OH

Howard A. Crystal, M.D.
Einstein College of Medicine, Yeshiva University, Bronx, NY

Zita DeFries, M.D.
private practice, New York, NY

Jennifer Egert, B.A.
Association for the Help of Retarded Children, New York, NY

John Fogelman, M.D.
St. Luke's/Roosevelt Hospital, New York, NY

Nancy Foldvary, D.O.
Cleveland Clinic Foundation, Cleveland, OH

David Geldmacher, M.D.
Fairhill Center for Aging, University Hospitals, Cleveland, OH

Kevin MacColl, M.A.
Beth Israel Medical Center, New York, NY

Michael McKee, Ph.D.
Cleveland Clinic Foundation, Cleveland, OH

Harriet N. Mischel, Ph.D.
private practice, New York, NY

German Nino-Murcia, M.D.
Stanford Sleep Medicine and Neurosciences Institute, Stanford, CA

Pat Pantone, Ph.D.
St. Luke's/Roosevelt Hospital Center, New York, NY

Steve Rasmussen, M.D.
Butler Hospital, Brown University, Providence, RI

Sharon Silver-Regent, Ph.D.
private practice, New York, NY

David Spiegel, M.D.
Stanford University Medical Center, Stanford, CA

Andrea Spungen, M.A.
Barnard College, New York, NY

B. Timothy Walsh, M.D.
Columbia University Medical Center,
New York State Psychiatric Institute, New York, NY

Fred Zimring, Ph.D.
Case Western Reserve University, Cleveland, OH

At McGraw-Hill, I thank Jane Acheson and John Wannemacher for their patience, expertise, and professionalism.

WORRIED SICK

PRESENTING COMPLAINT

Terry is a 31-year-old man living in Washington, D.C. At his first therapy session (often called the "initial interview" or "psychiatric/psychological evaluation"), he was dressed in clean but rather shabby "college clothes" (a t-shirt, jeans, and an old pullover jacket). Terry's manner and posture revealed that he was very apprehensive about therapy; his eyes nervously scanned the interview room, and he held himself stiffly rigid while talking, his speech was barely audible and marked by hesitations and a wavering tone. After some brief introductions, Terry and the therapist each took a scat. The therapist began the session by asking, "What brings you here today?"

Terry's reply was very rapid and forced. He stated that his problems began during his medial residency after graduating from medical school. "Oh, you're a doctor, then?" interjected the therapist. Terry seemed distracted—even thrown off—by her question. She realized that he felt pressured to describe his problems, and she decided to back off and let him tell his story without interrupting. Terry soon regained his train of thought and returned to his narrative. Being an internal medicine resident involved constant pressure and responsibilities. The schedule, involving 36-hour on-call periods, daily 6:00 a.m. rounds, and constant emergencies, was grueling and exhausting. Gradually he began to notice that he and his fellow residents were making a number of small errors and oversights in the care they provided their patients. Although he knew these were fairly common and relatively minor, still he found himself ruminating about his lapses. He began to hesitate in making decisions for fear of making some catastrophic mistake. His anxieties steadily worsened until he began calling in sick and avoiding particularly stressful situations at the hospital. As a result he was not completing many of the assignments given to him by the chief resident, who threatened to report him to the

1

program director. As time wore on, Terry's performance continued to decline, and by the end of the year he was threatened with dismissal from his program. He resigned at the end of the year.

Before his resignation he began making plans to be transferred to a less demanding program. With some help from his physican father and with some luck, he was accepted into a hospital in Washington, D.C. His second-year residency was indeed less demanding than the first, and he felt that perhaps he could manage it. After a few months, though, Terry again felt an overwhelming dread of making some terrible mistake, and he had to quit the second program after six months. He then began to work in a less stressful position as a research fellow for the Food and Drug Administration (FDA). Even in this relatively relaxed atmosphere, Terry found that he still had great difficulty carrying out his duties. He found that he could not handle any negative feelings at work, and he again began missing work to avoid trouble. Terry's contract with the FDA expired after six months and was not renewed. At this time even the prospect of having to apply for another position produced terrible anxieties, and Terry decided to stop working and instead live off a trust fund set up by his grandfather. For the last two years he has been supported by this trust fund and his girlfriend. With open self-criticism, Terry acknowledges that she pays "more than her share."

Besides crippling his career, Terry's incapacitating anxieties have interfered with his relationships. For one thing, he has avoided visiting his parents for the last three years. He states that his parents' poor opinions of him (particularly his father's) make going home "out of the question." He also confesses that he avoids discussing any potentially controversial subject with his girlfriend for fear that he may cause an irreconcilable rift. As Terry puts it, "I stay away from anything touchy because I don't want to say something wrong and blow it [the relationship]. Then what'll I do?" Even routine tasks, such as washing his clothes, shopping for groceries, and writing letters to friends are impossible to accomplish for fear that some small step may be bungled or overlooked. Terry freely acknowledges that his fears are exaggerated and irrational.

After some gentle prodding, he admits that he is an intelligent young man who should be successful. Nevertheless, he feels utterly unable to overcome his anxieties, and he takes great pains to avoid situations that may bring them on. His problems have left him feeling utterly worthless.

Along with these self-critical anxieties, Terry reports a number of somatic symptoms. He is very tense; he always feels nervous or "keyed up" and is easily distracted and irritated by minor problems. He complains of frequent throbbing headaches, annoying pains in his back and neck, and an almost constant feeling of fatigue. On occasion he experiences brief periods of acute anxiety in which he suffers from a shortness of breath, a wildly racing heartbeat, profuse sweating, and mild dizziness. These panicky feelings tend to come on when some feared situation (e.g., having to make a decision or having to confront his girlfriend) cannot be avoided. He states that these symptoms first emerged during his first residency and have gradually intensified over the past few years.

Terry began traditional psychodynamic psychotherapy soon after he lost his job with the FDA. He reports that this therapy was very complex and involved, which he found impressive in many ways. In particular, he says that his therapeutic experience gave him two important insights into the underlying causes of his paralyzing anxieties and low self-esteem: first, his parents' expectations of him were too high and he always felt a great pressure to be perfect in their eyes, and, second, the teasing he received from his peers as a child has made him self-conscious about his weaknesses. Although Terry felt that these insights were valid, they did not seem to bring about any significant change in his behavior. A friend suggested that Terry might benefit from a more direct form of psychotherapy and referred him to a cognitive-behavioral therapist.

PERSONAL HISTORY

Terry grew up in a small town in central Ohio. His father is a general practitioner in town and is on the staff of the county hospital. Terry's mother was an elementary school teacher until she quit her job when his older sister was born. After his younger sister was diagnosed as mentally retarded, however, his mother took night courses at Ohio State University to receive training in teaching special needs children. She is now employed in the county's MR/DD (mental retardation/developmentally delayed) program.

Terry says that his older sister is a disappointment to their parents. After getting average grades at a small local college and working for several years as a paralegal, she now attends a small, little-known law school. Terry describes her as "not too bright." His father criticizes her for not getting into a more prestigious law school. Part of his father's anger, Terry speculates, stems from frustration at being stuck in a routine medical position in a small town. His younger sister lives at home and works at a sheltered workshop for mentally retarded adults. According to Terry, his mother's training has enabled her to cope fairly well with the burdens of supporting a disabled child. He describes his father as coping with her retardation by focusing on his career and spending as much time away from home as possible.

According to Terry, his father wrote off his sisters early on and focused on Terry to be the success of the family. And Terry worked hard to fulfill this expectation. He had always earned excellent grades in school; in fact, he won a full scholarship at Northwestern University for his undergraduate education and a partial scholarship for his training at Harvard Medical School. He had always considered himself to be a good student. He enjoyed studying, even in the difficult, competitive atmosphere of medical school. He never experienced significant failure until his residencies, where for the first time he began to fear his own fallibility and to avoid anxiety-provoking situations.

CONCEPTUALIZATION AND TREATMENT

Terry is a very intelligent and articulate young man who appears to be much more competent and capable than he presents himself to be. He shows no evidence of a psychotic disorder. He seems willing, even pressured, to discuss his problems, and he seems highly motivated toward reducing them. Sometimes people's initial complaints don't really describe their underlying disorder, either because they distort their descriptions or are unaware of their real problems. But Terry seems to have a good awareness of his situation and to truly want help, and so the therapist thought it reasonable to accept his complaints at face value.

Terry's primary problem involves an excessive and unwarranted apprehension about his own fallibility, perhaps motivated by his irrational need to perform every activity perfectly, no matter how trivial. This overriding fear has crippled his occupational and social functioning as well as his ability to perform a variety of routine, everyday tasks. This anxiety is also manifested by a number of physiological symptoms, including constant vigilance, distractibility, and irritability; pervasive muscle tension; and autonomic hyperactivity, as expressed by his occasional panicky feelings. He also complains of feeling depressed and worthless.

Terry's symptoms clearly fit the *DSM-IV-TR* criteria for generalized anxiety disorder, usually abbreviated GAD. People with this disorder suffer from pervasive, long-standing, and uncontrollable feelings of dread or worry that involve a number of major life activities (career, marriage, parenting, etc.). The focus of these anxieties is much broader than is the case with more circumscribed anxiety disorders such as panic disorder or simple phobia. A diagnosis of GAD requires that the anxiety is not just the result of some other Axis I diagnosis. In Terry's case, he feels depressed as well as anxious, but his anxiety is pervasive and not solely about being depressed. In addition, people with GAD display somatic signs of their apprehension, including muscle tension, autonomic hyperactivity, fatigue, and irritability. Terry clearly fits this picture.

Terry's therapy can be organized as a process involving four general steps. The therapist's first aim was to establish rapport with her client. To establish a better working relationship with Terry, she attempted to make him feel comfortable with her. This is no easy task with someone as tense and anxious as Terry. She started by explaining her treatment approach. Because cognitive-behavioral therapy requires much more direct, active participation than initially supposed by many clients (particularly those like Terry who have a history of psychodynamic treatment), it is important that the client be made fully aware of what to expect. The therapist also gave Terry encouragement that his disorder was treatable with cognitive-behavioral therapy. It is important to establish this basis of hope to foster the client's expectations for change.

The second step was to have Terry form goals for his therapy. Ideally these goals would involve some specific behaviors or attitudes. It is more effective to formulate concrete plans that address some particular feared situation, such as "I want to send my résumé to 50 prospective employers," than more general aims such as "I want to get back to work." Like most clients with GAD, though, Terry at first proposed goals that were quite vague and unfocused. He wanted to start working, to get along with his parents better, and to "not be so anxious about things." At first these general goals are adequate; they were better defined as therapy progressed. In the beginning it is more important point is to have the client formulate *some* goals and engage in therapy. Overly general ones can always be put into more specific behavioral contexts later on.

Third, relaxation training is suggested for clients who show a great deal of physical tension. Therapists have developed relaxation techniques that specifically address a client's dysfunctional cognitions, muscular tension, and autonomic hyperactivity. When he began therapy, Terry showed a variety of physical manifestations of tension. Having been trained in medicine, he was willing to try relaxation techniques that involved physiological elements.

The fourth step in therapy was a review by Terry and the therapist of the issues and goals Terry had targeted. By going over his initial complaints and plans, both the therapist and the client are assured that they understand each other fully. In addition, this review allows the client, with the aid of the therapist, to put vague initial goals into more specific and workable terms.

Therapy began by first discussing the specific issues that were of immediate concern to Terry. These topics were not necessarily a central part of Terry's goals. For example, Terry's first few sessions of therapy focused on a variety of distinct problems, including his inability to buy a suit, his anxiety concerning needed dental work, and his dread of an upcoming visit to his parents. These loosely related issues were dealt with on a problem-by-problem basis, a process the therapist referred to as "putting out fires." This troubleshooting approach is employed for several reasons. First, cognitive-behavioral therapy is most effective if therapeutic issues are specified and well defined; individual psychological "fires" are particularly suited to this. Second, the client's enthusiasm for therapy and belief in the effectiveness of treatment is likely to be increased by initial success experiences, especially problem areas that are of immediate interest to the client. Third, although these issues do not appear to be closely related, for the most part they share a common foundation: they are all indications of Terry's tendency to avoid situations that carry a possibility of failure, however inconsequential. Over time, clients are expected to integrate these isolated issues and generalize their therapeutic gains to other areas of their lives.

The first topic Terry wanted to discuss was his inability to buy himself a suit. It had been years since Terry had shopped for clothes; he contented himself with wearing worn jeans and t-shirts. Several months ago, Terry's girlfriend made plans for the two of them to take a vacation to Boston to visit her sister. As a part of the preparation for this trip, she asked him to buy some new clothes, including "at least one decent suit." He thought about buying a suit on several occasions, but every time he went shopping he was over-whelmed by the prospect of having to pick one out. He would begin shaking and sweating even as he approached a clothing store. Terry explained that he hated shopping for clothes, especially suits, because he was convinced that he would not be able to pick out the right one. Not only would he waste his money, but everyone else would see his failure. To be at all acceptable, the suit had to be just the right color, just the right material, just the right cut, just the right price, and so on. It also had to be practical—appropriate for every possible occasion, from a sightseeing tour to a funeral. The prospect of buying the "wrong suit" made him so anxious that he could not bring himself to even enter a clothing store.

The therapist began by having Terry clarify exactly what he was and was not capable of. She then gave him clear assignments that she judged he would be able to accomplish successfully. These assignments started off with small steps that Terry thought he could do easily; gradually these steps became more and more complicated and difficult. The following segment of a therapy session illustrates this process:

> **Terry:** You see, I just can't go through with it [buying a suit].
>
> **Therapist:** Do you mean you are unable to, or that you'd rather avoid the whole thing?
>
> **Terry:** What do you mean?
>
> **Therapist:** Well, if I held a gun to your head, would you be able to go to the clothing store?
>
> **Terry:** Well, yeah, I suppose so.
>
> **Therapist:** So you are physically able to walk into a clothing store, right?
>
> **Terry:** Yeah, I guess I am.
>
> **Therapist:** OK. I want you to go to at least two clothing stores on your way home today. All right?
>
> **Terry:** The mall's too far away. I couldn't possibly make it to day.

Therapist: There's no need to go to the mall. There are at least five good clothing stores right around here; three are on this street.

Terry: Well, they're too expensive.

Therapist: No, not really. I've shopped at most of them, and the prices are actually better than at the mall.

Terry: I really don't know if I'll have the time.

Therapist: It'll take a half an hour at most. Come on, Terry, no more excuses. I want you to go to two stores. Today.

Terry: But what if I buy the wrong suit?

Therapist: You don't need to buy anything. Just walk into two stores. That's it. If you feel comfortable with that, then start browsing. You might want to try one or two suits on. But for today, I just want you to take the first step and go to two stores. Agreed?

Terry: Well, all right.

At the next session Terry stated that he had followed the therapist's directions and had gone to a store down the street from her office. After he went to the first store, he found that looking for a suit was not as difficult as he had expected. In fact, he actually went to three stores and bought two suits. Unfortunately, Terry was not able to enjoy his success for long. Several weeks ago his driver's license expired. He felt very anxious about driving with his expired license, and he knew that he had to get his license renewed, which involved taking a simple written test of basic traffic regulations. He had gotten a copy of the driver's manual and had planned to go over it several times, but each time he was struck with a terrible fear that he might miss some vital piece of information and fail his test. Terry admitted that his worries were irrational. He had missed no more than a single question on any driving test before. He realized that the test was very basic and that the chances of his actually failing the test were very remote, even if he did not study the manual at all. Still, he could not bring himself to study the manual, and the thought of taking the test terrified him.

Again, the therapist approached the problem directly and made concrete suggestions. First, she reassured him that he was a very intelligent person who graduated from medical school; he would have no trouble passing a simple driving test, even without reading the manual. Nevertheless, she thought that the manual would be reassuring. She suggested different ways to get him to read it, such as skimming it or just reading every other page. She explained that failing the exam was not the end of the world; even on the slight chance that he did fail the exam, he would still have two other opportunities to retake it. Finally, she reminded him that it was worse to be stopped while driving with an expired license than to just go ahead and take the test. This last warning was meant to propel Terry to action, but it was a bit risky; it could have been stopped him from driving altogether to avoid a ticket. When he mentioned this, the therapist reassured him that driving with a license that expired only a few weeks ago would most likely get him only a warning. At worst, he would have to pay a small fine. As time wore on, however, trying to explain that he just forgot about his license would become less and less credible. The time to take his test was now.

Again Terry followed the therapist's instructions. He read over the manual carefully and tried not to be too concerned if he did not remember every fact. Following her directions, if he felt that he could not remember some information from any particular page, he would consciously limit himself to skimming that page once. At the next session he reported, as expected, that he had passed his test without missing a question. But just like the previous session, however, his accomplishment was darkened by another problem that came up during the week.

Another source of apprehension concerned writing a letter to an old roommate from college. They had exchanged correspondence for years, but Terry had not responded to this friend's last three letters for fear that he might look foolish through some mistake in his grammar or spelling. He worried that the friend, who was a journalist, would then lose respect for him. Terry's anxieties were heightened after his friend's last letter. In it, the friend jokingly wondered whether Terry had forgotten how to write. This comment made Terry wonder if he had indeed lost his ability to compose a letter that would be acceptable to his friend. Like everything else, his therapist had Terry approach this problem in gradual steps. First, he was to make a brief outline of what he would put in a letter. Next, he was to write a letter that they could go over during the next session. As was the case with shopping for a suit and renewing his license, Terry found that just starting an avoided activity greatly diminished his apprehensions, and he finished and sent the letter without ever showing it to the therapist.

Terry found that after each fire was put out, he felt much less anxiety about that topic the next time he attempted it. It also required fewer steps to complete these tasks. After several sessions of putting out fires, Terry's therapy began to focus on more global interpersonal issues. At one session Terry discussed his fears that his girlfriend was planning to leave him. During the previous week she said that a special project came up at work (she worked in an architectural firm) and that they would have to postpone their vacation to Boston for a month. Terry, who constantly harbored fears that she would end their relationship, took this as a sign that she was ready to leave him. He asked the therapist what he could do to make her stay. The therapist told him that no one could guarantee that their relationship would last forever and began to discuss whether it was likely that Terry's fears were accurate. Initially Terry refused to discuss this possibility, saying "Don't tell me anything about her leaving. I don't want to hear it!" His therapist

11

persisted, however, and reminded him of the importance of not avoiding important topics. Over the next two sessions he gradually became able to discuss the possibility of her leaving him. He even made some plans if indeed this occurred. But like most of his worries, this too was for nothing. She finished her project, and they went to Boston on the postponed date.

While they were in Boston, Terry's mother fell and broke her hip. When his father asked when Terry would be coming to visit, Terry made a feeble excuse about his schedule. He knew he was expected to visit her, but he dreaded going home and interacting with his parents, particularly his father, who would undoubtedly ask him about what he has been doing over the past few years. He pleaded with his therapist, "Tell me what to say to them!"

The therapist engaged Terry in a role-playing exercise. First, she instructed him to enact his father while she modeled effective responses to his father's comments and criticisms. Terry was told to pay close attention to her while she modeled these behaviors; he was to remember her posture, the color of her blouse, everything. These details were not important in themselves; they were meant to give Terry a clear, visual reference that would help him remember the modeled responses. After going over several responses, the roles were changed. Now the therapist enacted the role of Terry's father, and Terry discussed possible responses from his own viewpoint. Because it was felt that maintaining a good interaction with his parents was just as important as dealing with a bad interaction, Terry practiced responding to many different types of comments, both positive and negative.

When Terry returned from Ohio, he reported that his father was indeed as critical as he had feared. His father was very disappointed that he had given up a career in medicine, and he kept asking Terry what he had been doing for the past three years. His father felt that every man should at least support himself by the time he was finished with his education. Although these interactions made Terry very anxious, he was able to maintain control over his feelings and was able to stay in the family home for the entire 10-day visit. Terry stated that his interactions with his mother and older sister were generally positive. He found, somewhat to his surprise, that he really enjoyed their company. Although he still felt nervous about visiting his parents, he felt that he could have an adequate interaction with them and decided not to wait so long before visiting them again. (Six months later Terry was more comfortable about discussing a visit with his parents, but he had not actually visited them again.)

Terry felt that much of his father's disappointment was justified, and the next focus of therapy was for Terry to apply for jobs. When Terry began therapy, getting back to work was a goal, although in reality he seemed perfectly happy to keep living off the trust fund. But now Terry felt enough confidence to begin a true job search.

Like every other aspect of therapy, Terry and his therapist approached this task one step at a time. First, they discussed the sorts of jobs he would be interested in and capable of performing. Terry's estimations of his own abilities were consistently lower than his therapist's. He also wanted to avoid any job that involved pressure and responsibility. At first, he thought of becoming a library researcher for some government agency. His therapist, who also thought it wise to avoid any high-pressure positions, told him that he could probably do better, perhaps something that would enable him to use his medical training. They finally decided that he should seek employment that involved medical issues but was outside a hospital or clinic setting. The therapist's instructions were concrete and firm: by the next week he was to have his résumé compiled, and one week later he was to have it printed. She then directed him to send out at least 10 applications per week until he heard something. During this time they rehearsed possible interview questions through role-playing. After eight weeks (and by making use of a few old contacts), he was offered a part-time position at the Food and Drug Administration as a research assistant. He found that he enjoyed working and could do his job well. After six months he was offered a full-time staff position.

Terry discontinued therapy at about the time that he was hired full time. His therapy had involved an eight-month process of directly approaching various psychological "fires" and learning to cope with his fears. With these success experiences, he was able to develop a sense of himself that was consistent with his actual abilities. Over the past few months he reported that his self-esteem had gradually improved and that his risk-avoidance habits were starting to decline. He still worried about performing various tasks and duties well, but he was now able to attempt these activities in spite of his apprehensions. Only rarely did his fears cause him to avoid these situations entirely. He was able to discuss possible negative consequences of his own and other people's actions. In short, although he stated that he still felt anxious about some situations, he felt that he was learning to control his fears. He felt better about himself and his work. Most noticeably, he was working steadily and routinely engaging in a wide variety of activities that he would not have even attempted just six months before.

PROGNOSIS

Terry's prognosis is positive. When he began therapy, he had very low self-esteem and very little confidence in his abilities to perform even the most trivial task. Consequently he avoided situations that involved any amount of pressure or responsibility. His constant fears of being embarrassed or rejected also interfered with his interpersonal relationships. Without treatment, it is possible that Terry would have become severely agoraphobic, that is, so overwhelmed by his anxieties that he would be unable to leave his home or interact with other people. At the very least, it is likely that his ability to carry out his day-to-day tasks and his ability to maintain his relationships with his family, friends, and girlfriend would have continued to deteriorate.

Terry has reversed this trend. His paralyzing anxieties are greatly diminished, and his avoidance behavior for the most part has ended. By encouraging him to face feared situations directly and in small increments, his therapy seems to have enabled him to approach a variety of previously avoided situations. In addition, he is able to apply this step-by-step approach to problem areas that were never directly discussed in therapy. He also has been able to integrate the therapeutic gains of these isolated tasks and make progress in his more global problems involving his interpersonal relationships and his career. In addition to his behavioral gains, Terry has also built up his self-esteem and self-confidence, as evidenced by a shift in his therapy goals. Broadly speaking, Terry's initial aim in therapy was to avoid any pain, rejection, or pressure in his career or his interpersonal relationships. Now, however, he is able to work through difficult tasks, and generally he avoids situations only if they may be unduly stressful. This shift appears to be a good indication that Terry will maintain his therapeutic gains.

ANXIETY RUSH

Earl Campbell was one of the greatest rushers in football history. As a running back for the Texas Longhorns, he was voted All Southwest Conference four times and won the Heisman Trophy in 1977. He was the first draft pick in the 1978 NFL draft and ended his first year in the pros by being elected Rookie of the Year and Most Valuable Player. He played in the Pro Bowl for seven consecutive years, and despite a relatively short pro career he is ranked tenth in career rushing yards. In 1991 he was enshrined in the Pro Football Hall of Fame. And oh yes, throughout his football career he suffered from Panic Disorder.

The following case is about someone who is in many ways similar to the all-star running back. He is a robust, athletic young man in his mid 20s. Like Earl Campbell, he is just about the last person one would suspect of having a crippling anxiety disorder.

PRESENTING COMPLAINT

Tom is a 26-year-old man living in Austin, Texas, Earl Campbell's hometown. Tom works for the gas company, investigating reported leaks, checking on installations, and generally spending his days driving around the Austin area responding to calls. To say he is physically fit is an understatement; he lifts weights, runs, bicycles, and swims most days in preparation for his hobby: competing in Iron Man competitions. He has been married for three years and is the father of a 12-month-old son. He would be in the prime of life—if only he could leave his home.

It all started about 3 months ago. Tom was driving on the highway back from repairing a routine residential gas leak when WHAM! his heart was racing and seemingly beating out of his chest. He couldn't breathe, and he felt like someone was standing on his chest. He was sweating, shaking, and nauseated. He was dizzy and faint, and felt his legs going numb. He had an intense sense of dread; he just knew he was having a heart attack and would die. He found himself saying what everyone always said, "Why me?!?" Somehow he pulled off the road and called 911 from his truck. The EMS team arrived in about five minutes and rushed him to Southwest General, which fortunately for him is one of the best heart hospitals in the country.

The emergency doctor who examined him saw a strapping young man who was pale, sweaty, and shaking. His breathing was shallow and his pulse was elevated, but otherwise there was really nothing wrong with him. His EKG (electrocardiogram—a printout of his heartbeat used to detect cardiac abnormalities) confirmed that his heart was perfectly normal, aside from the fact that it was probably the healthiest heart that ever came through those emergency doors! Tom's wife was called from the ambulance, and she met him at the hospital just as the exam was ending. The doctor seemed relaxed and jovial. "Well, your heart's fine. It looks like you just had a little anxiety. Nothing to worry about. Do you have any problems with alcohol or drug use? No, I didn't think so. OK. Here's a prescription for Ativan. Take one if you feel another anxiety attack coming on. But no more than three a day. OK? Well, I've got to get going!"

What the hell was that? Tom didn't know whether to be relieved or appalled. It was the worst experience he had every had, and what did the doctor say? "A little anxiety"? "Nothing to worry about"? And what was that about drinking and drugs? Tom had always avoided taking any kind of drug, and he didn't like the idea of taking this Ativan stuff. But he didn't want to go through an episode like that again, so he picked up the prescription, just in case.

Tom didn't know what to tell his supervisor other than he felt chest pains but was OK. This made him feel more than a little foolish, and his supervisor had his doubts too. For the next several days, he avoided exercising because he didn't want to get his heart racing again. But after two weeks went by and nothing happened, he went back to his workout routine. Then one Wednesday evening, after he finished his workout and the dishes, and after Pam had put Charlie to sleep, they sat down to watch the Ranger game and relax.

About 20 minutes later, Pam noticed a wild look in Tom's eyes. He was sweating and shaking, and he seemed to be hyperventilating. "Dammit! I knew he missed something!" She rushed him back to the hospital, calling a neighbor to watch Charlie while she was on her way. As they pulled up to the Emergency Department door, Tom could barely walk. But he remembered muttering, "I hope they don't give me that same quack."

They didn't. This time he was examined by a resident who seemed even younger than Tom. She performed the same exam, administered the same tests, and came up with the same clean EKG. The doctor from Tom's first visit, an attending, then stopped by to check over the resident's work and sign off on the chart. "So, you're back with us, I see. You haven't been taking that Ativan, have you? Well, give it a try." And with a wink, he was gone.

Now Tom was really confused. And scared. These attacks could come at any time. What if they happened at work, while he was trying to fix some gas leak. KABOOM! What if it happened during one of his competitions. Everyone else is running, and he's just hunched over there, clutching his heart and gasping for air. Even going to the store can be a nightmare.

Two days later be bolted up from a dead sleep with his next attack. At least he knew to expect them now. But he had hoped that taking that medication would eliminate them. All it seemed to do was make him tired and a little groggy. Now, knowing he would have attacks even on the medication, he thought twice about going out, about working out, and gradually he began doing less and less. The attacks kept coming, not regularly, but they averaged about once a week, maybe more. The attacks in the daytime weren't as bad as the first few, but the nighttime ones were. He worried constantly about what he would do and what people would think of him having his attack. He had already stopped exercising, he missed one competition, and he began calling off work when the worries got too bad. After six weeks of attacks, he saw his doctor.

Tom was in luck. Just last week, his doctor had just given a public information presentation on panic disorder along with a psychologist from their group practice, so she recognized the symptoms immediately. She changed his antianxiety medication from Ativan to clonipramine (Klonopin). She explained that both are in the same chemical family, benzodiazepines, but Klonopin has a more gradual effect. This is crucial because panic attacks can be triggered by a rebound effect—they can be brought on when the medication wears off. She also prescribed paroxetine (Paxil), an SSRI antidepressant that is effective in treating panic attacks. She explained that the benzodiazepines act like a salve; they will reduce the symptoms of an attack, but they won't make the attack go away. The SSRIs, especially Paxil and Zoloft, actually prevent the attacks from happening. That sounded good to Tom. But the SSRIs tend to take a few weeks to start working—so Tom was to use the Klonopin in the interim, and then gradually taper off. She also referred him to the psychologist for cognitive-behavioral therapy.

Not in his wildest dreams (or perhaps nightmares) did Tom ever think he would end up in a shrink's office. He didn't know what to expect—so lie on a couch and talk about his parents? He was relieved that the psychologist seemed matter of fact and businesslike. She looked through the notes Tom's doctor wrote in his chart and said simply, "So, you get panic attacks. Let's get to work."

PERSONAL HISTORY

Tom is a local boy, born and raised in Austin. He has one older sister and two younger brothers. Both parents live nearby and are involved as proud new grandparents. He described his childhood as typical: no traumas, no abuse, no unusual experiences. Some drinking and a little marijuana use, but he never got much into drugs. He was a jock, playing split end/defensive back for the football team and running the 440 for the track team. After high school he joined the Air Force and spent 3 years hanging ordnance on bombers in Idaho. When he returned home a friend at the gas company got him into their training program, and he been working for them for over three years. Soon after he started working a mutual friend introduced him to Pam, and they were married a year later. They had a son 14 months later.

Tom was surprised—relieved but surprised—that the psychologist didn't seem particularly interested in his childhood or his parents. What she did seem to care about was whether anyone in his family had any mental problems, especially panic attacks, agoraphobia (fear of leaving the home), or any other anxiety issues. His mother was always a worrier, but she never had any treatment. And he heard about one of his aunts—his maternal grandmother's sister, he thinks, who was afraid to leave her house. Otherwise, nothing.

She also focused on his drinking and drug use. "What's with all the questions about alcohol?" he asked. She explained that benzodiazepines, like Ativan and Klonopin, work on the same receptor sites as alcohol. If the person has two drinks while taking one of these drugs, it's like having ten drinks. Also, benzodiazepines are naturally addicting, so they would be contraindicated for anyone with a history of drinking or drug problems.

"I don't mean to be mean or anything, but I'm wondering," asked Tom, "if I have the medication, why do I need to see you?" "That's a good question," she responded, not offended at all. "I'm here to give you cognitive strategies, that is, changes in the way you think, that will help you cope with your attacks you have and reduce the number of your attacks as quickly as possible. Research shows that the best treatment is a combination of medications and therapy."

CONCEPTUALIZATION AND TREATMENT

For Tom's therapist, "Let's get to work" was a fairly straightforward process. First of all, the diagnosis was clear-cut: Panic Disorder with Agoraphobia.

DSM-IV-TR criteria specify a panic attack as "a discrete period of intense fear or discomfort" which begins suddenly and peaks within 10 minutes. These attacks include a variety of subjective feelings of: the heart pounding (palpitations) or racing (tachycardia), chest pain, chest pressure, shortness of breath, choking or smothering, sweating, chills or hot flushes, shaking, numbness or tingling, nausea, and various ideas of dread, such as fears that one is dying, going crazy, or has lost touch with oneself (depersonalization) or the environment (derealization). Tom felt most of these symptoms in the course of his attacks.

But a panic attack alone is not a disorder. Panic becomes Panic Disorder when there are recurrent attacks, and the person does any of the following: worries about having future attacks, worries that the attacks might be harmful in some way (heart attack, going crazy, etc.), or changes behavior because of the attacks. Tom did all three.

Finally, DSM-IV-TR asks whether Panic Disorder is associated with Agoraphobia. This is an anxiety condition where the person fears being in places where they may be embarrassed and cannot escape or where they may be unable to get help, and the person begins to avoid these places because of embarrassment, fear, or just because it feels unsafe. In extreme cases, everywhere except one's own home is deemed unsafe, and the agoraphobic becomes a person under house arrest, unable to leave their home. Although Tom is not at this stage, he certainly is showing signs agoraphobia by avoiding outings and calling off work.

The first step in Tom's psychotherapy was psycho-education to inform him of the likely times when panic attacks will strike. Ironically, most panic attacks happen in situations where the person is relaxing, or where their mind is not fully engaged in some immediate activitiy but instead has a chance to dwell on other ideas. Common situations where panic attacks strike are sleeping, relaxing with friends, watching TV, worship services, driving on the highway (but rarely around town), and shopping. This is good news because it gave Tom confidence that a panic attack will *not* strike at work, so there is no need to avoid his job. A second element in psychoeducation is explain the nature of panic attacks so that he can understand that although the panic symptoms are horrendous to experience, they pose no real health problems or behavior risks, and they usually disperse within 30 minutes. Other people rarely notice when someone is having an attack, so there's little risk of embarrassment. Also, although panic attacks frequently occur when people drive on the highway, there have been almost no instances of any accidents. Although the person feels completely out of control, this is obviously not the case. Just this psychoeducation did wonders toward relieving Tom's anxieties and giving him confidence to just work through them.

The next step in Tom's treatment was to counter his agoraphobic avoidance. Like any behavioral phobia treatment, this stage of his therapy consisted of two elements: cue exposure and response prevention. Cue exposure means having him actively enter feared situations. For example, for the past several weeks Tom has avoided his physical workouts for fear of elevating his pulse and breathing. His physical fitness is a big part of his self-identification, and this avoidance poses a devastating loss for him. The therapist instructed Tom in a process of interoceptive exposure. Interoception refers to an awareness of internal stimuli, like breathing patterns and heart rate. Beginning slowly and then advancing steadily, she got Tom used to an elevated heart rate and breathing rate under conditions where he felt safe. In his case, she had him use the staircase in the medical building. First he would walk up and down a flight, then two flights, then working toward all five. Next he did the same, but running instead of walking. In this way, he was exposed to feared cues and not allowed to avoid them, all under controlled, safe conditions.

Finally, the therapist probed Tom for any cognitive meaning that may underlie his symptoms. One question most therapists have in the back of their minds is "why now?" Sometimes panic can result from a repression of emotions such as fear or anger that the person is unable or unwilling to deal with openly. Often pent-up resentment or worries about incompetence are associated with the panic attacks. In discussions with Tom, no real cognitive issues emerged.

Tom showed dramatic improvement over the eight weekly sessions of his therapy. During the first two weeks, he experienced blunted panic attacks. That is, he felt an attack coming on, but it seemed to lose steam before it became really intense. After that, he experienced no attacks at all. He has not missed work since the first session, and over the course of therapy he returned to all of his previous activities.

In the course of his therapy, Tom gradually decreased his use of Klonopin and had discontinued completely as of the sixth week. He remained on Paxil for another four months, but he complained that he had been having sexual side effects (in his case, trouble maintain erections), and Paxil was gradually withdrawn over the next six weeks.

PROGNOSIS

There is a saying that medication helps in the short term, whereas psychotherapy helps over the long term. In other words, medications help reduce symptoms quickly, and therapy helps prevent relapse. This seemed to be the case with Tom. About a year after therapy, while taking his son to their doctor, Tom reported that he had had only a few instances of increased anxiety, but nothing approaching a full-blown panic attack.

In general, people who suffer from Panic Disorder, with or without Agoraphobia, tend to be a mixed group. DSM-IV-TR reports that most respond well to therapy initially. Over the next several years, about a third remain free of symptoms, about half have some recurring symptoms but they are much reduced and generally manageable, and about one-fifth never respond or get worse. Tom will probably be in the middle group, one who suffers intermittent anxiety at various points in his life, but these will likely be manageable anxiety pangs rather than full-blown attacks. Also, he is confident that medications and behavioral therapies are available should he need them in the future. Although this isn't complete remission, this is a great improvement over his symptoms before therapy, and he's happy for the change.

9-11 WILL NOT BE FORGOTTON

PRESENTING COMPLAINT

Abbey half-ran, half-jumped her way down the darkened stairs for 25 flights. She clutched the handrail in quick, grabbing motions to make sure she didn't fall. She was relieved to make it to the ground floor. Despite the choking smoke, the dust, and the hurried excitement of everyone rushing to get out, the lobby was oddly quiet and sunny. She didn't know why the building was being evacuated; in the stairwell she heard excited talk of terrorists, bombs, fire, even planes crashing into the big towers next door, crazy talk. Whatever it was, she was almost out now. With an immense sense of relief bordering on giddiness, she moved through the main doors that led outside to safety. She would be OK! Then, within an instant, BAM! Dazed, she found herself sitting down on the pavement, blankly trying to put together what had just happened. She was covered with blood . . . Oh, God, a bomb! She tested her feet and found that she could stand. She could use her arms, she could hear, she could see. She seemed to be OK. She looked around, and everyone seemed to be looking up. *Up?* She followed their faces, and she saw an awesome sight. Tower two, looming up over them, was on fire with thick, black smoke was billowing out. She noticed that people's stares were following things that were falling. Things were falling out of the tower. *That* was it. Something fell right next to her and knocked her down. But what? A desk? Glass? No, she wasn't hurt or cut, but why all the blood? Then, with a sickening realization, she knew what must've happened. These weren't things falling down, these were people jumping to escape the fire. Then she couldn't help looking down, and what she saw confirmed her worst fears. There was the blood spatter, red pulp of torn flesh, the bones, the belt and fabric shreds. A man had jumped out of God knows what floor, missed her by less than a foot, and had exploded on impact at her feet.

Case 3

Abbey was in her room in her parents house now, and her father was gently rubbing her arm to wake her up. She was shaking and drenched in a cold sweat. Her mother was there too, standing in the doorway with a worried look on her face. Abbey knew they must have been woken up by her screams, yet again. Here she was, eight months later, and that day never left her. A transfer to Chicago hadn't helped, and now the final retreat to her childhood home in Nashville wasn't helping either. About a month ago she took a medical leave from the company and moved back to her hometown, hoping the peace and quiet would help. If anything, it was worse. She dreamed of her harrowing experience every night, and visions of the catastrophe haunted her in the daytime. She couldn't sleep, couldn't eat, couldn't keep her mind on anything. How long was this going to last? The radio she kept on all night softly played the sad voice of country singer Alan Jackson: *Where were you when the world stopped turning, that September day?* Oh, if she could only forget!

What was today, Wednesday? Oh yeah, she had that appointment with a psychologist. She prayed that that would help.

PERSONAL HISTORY

Abbey is an intelligent, hard-working single 26-year-old who until recently was a rising stockbroker for a major national investment firm. She threw herself into her work, and like many young people in her situation, career took precedence over relationships.

She had always excelled at school and worked hard at her many extracurricular activities. And she had always been successful, first at Vanderbilt for her BA, then at Wharton for her MBA. Her only sibling was her brother, three years older, who in his own way was just as focused and dedicated as she was. He was a Navy pilot who was now stationed in the Middle East.

Abbey's parents were, in a word, solid. Her father was a professor of history at Vanderbilt, and her mother was a hospital administrator. As far as she could tell, they had a stable, loving marriage. She laughed when asked if there was any child abuse or domestic violence in the home, "Oh, no, never," she responded, "They're my rocks. My foundation."

They accompanied Abbey to her initial session, and one could see why she'd feel that way. "Solid" was the word that seemed to describe them. When they were asked to describe their daughter's symptoms from their perspective, they could add little to what she said herself. The only area where their views diverged from Abbey's was in describing past anxiety. Abbey denied any past anxiety or depression, but her parents remember her worrying about her grades and her many other duties. She would often stay up until midnight, 1:00 a.m. to make sure everything was done just right. Other than this perfectionism, they could add nothing in the way of any family psychiatric history or past psychiatric history preceding 9-11.

Post-9-11 was a different story. Abbey remembers little from that day. Somehow she got back to her apartment on the Upper West Side and was able to call her parents, who naturally were worried sick. She stayed home most of the next week, watching mesmerized as the airliner rammed the second tower, over and over again. With the New York offices in shambles, there was little for her to do for the next few days, and she did little, only leaving her apartment twice for some items at the corner store. After the first day she kept the TV off, wanting to avoid thinking about that morning. For most people, the victims were just anonymous statistics, but Abbey knew many people who were killed that morning, and she lost many close friends.

She was offered a transfer to the Chicago office late that week, and she eagerly accepted and moved before the end of the month. She thought being away from New York would help, but The Jump, as she called it, kept playing in her mind without letup.

Case 3

CONCEPTUALIZATION AND TREATMENT

It is not surprising that people who experience frightening events develop problems with anxiety, and a diagnosis of Adjustment Disorder with Anxiety is given where the anxiety reaction interferes with the person's daily living. However, people's reactions can be much stronger in cases where the precipitating event is a full-blown trauma, especially if it is personally threatening. In these cases, anxiety can be overwhelming. The *DSM-IV-TR* diagnosis of Post-Traumatic Stress Disorder (PTSD) involves a cluster of anxious symptoms occurring after the person has been exposed to a traumatic event that resulted in feelings of horror, helplessness, or fear. One aspect involves re-experiencing the event through dreams, flashbacks, feeling the event were recurring, and psychological or physical distress at reminders of the event. A second aspect relates to efforts to avoid memories of the trauma, such as purposely avoiding thoughts or actions that may remind the person of the event, losing interest in the event or in other people, forgetting, diminished emotions, pessimism regarding a shortened future. Third, the person experiences increased arousal in the form of being easily startled, always looking out for dangers, poor concentration, irritability, or insomnia. Finally, the duration and timing of events plays an important role in the diagnosis: symptoms experienced for less than one month are diagnosed as an Acute Stress Disorder; symptoms that last over one month is PTSD. Within PTSD, suffering symptoms from one to three months is acute PTSD, problems lasting more than three months is chronic PTSD. Finally, people with a delayed onset PTSD don't experience any recognizable symptoms right away, but the symptoms emerge later. Sometimes it is as recently as six months later, sometimes it is years later. Abbey clearly met the criteria for PTSD; the pattern of her symptoms would categorize her as suffering chronic PTSD.

Abbey's psychologist thought that a three-part approach utilizing medication, group therapy, and individual therapy would be most beneficial in her case. He referred her to a local psychiatrist he often worked with, and she put Abbey on a combination of the SSRI sertraline (Zoloft) to be taken in the morning and the novel antidepressant trazodone at bedtime. After the first week, the dose of each was increased from 50 to 100 mg. Although both medications are approved by the FDA as antidepressants, they are used for different reasons. SSRIs tend to reduce anxious feelings, especially anxious ruminations. Trazodone (whose trade name is Desyrel, but by some quirk professionals always seem to refer to it by its chemical name trazodone) is prescribed primarily to promote sleep. Abbey experienced increased night sweats and anxious agitation, and she switched her SSRI escitalopram oxalate (Lexapro), and these symptoms subsided. People's reactions to medications, especially SSRIs, are highly variable; how they react to one does not predict how they may react to another. After about 3 weeks, Abbey began to feel the Lexipro "kick in," and her anxious symptoms were reduced significantly.

The second part of her therapy involved group sessions. If Abbey had stayed in New York, there would have been numerous PTSD groups solely devoted to the World Trade Center attack, in the same way that many VA hospitals offer groups composed entirely of Vietnam veterans. However, here in Nashville any PTSD group would include people who suffered from a variety of traumas. Abbey's group included two women who had been raped, one Vietnam vet, one witness to a murder, one victim of child abuse, one man whose wife had died in a car accident, and Abbey.

The first order of business in the group was to reduce the avoidance by addressing the traumas directly. Gently, and with support, group members were led to discuss their situations in as much detail as they could tolerate. As the group sessions went on, members generally were able to provide more detail.

A second element of the group experience was to address the intense anger that almost always accompanies a traumatic event. As it turned out, it was relatively easy for the members of this group to identify a target for their angry feelings. Sometimes the nature of the traumatic event makes it difficult to identity any culprit; storms, earthquakes, building collapses, diseases all may lead to PTSD.

29

Sometimes these victims blame God or fate for their excruciating pain. Abbey had no such trouble here; she could identify 19 men and their terrorist leader as objects of her inner wrath. The war in Afghanistan helped somewhat to alleviate her feelings of helplessness.

Third, the group functioned to show support for the individual members, both by making it clear that others suffered anxiety as well, and also by giving members encouragement and hope for better times in the future.

The group utilized many different techniques and materials. The one that affected Abbey most deeply was watching a videotape of Rabbi Harold Kushner discuss his book *When Bad Things Happen to Good People* (1981). This, along with everything else, of course, helped her put her pain in perspective.

A third element of her treatment involved individual sessions with her psychologist. Given the nature of her problem as described when she made her appointment, he decided to utilize a technique pioneered by Francine Shapiro called Eye Movement Desensitization and Reprocessing (EMDR, Shapiro, 1995, 2002) as an important tool in his therapy.

Abbey's psychologist had several tasks at the first session. First, he needed to establish a safe, trusting therapeutic relationship with Abbey so she would feel comfortable working with him. Next, he discussed and demonstrated self-soothing techniques such as relaxation and deep breathing. As part of his history of her, he got a good sense of the exact memories and images that were bothering her, as well as her reactions to them. Finally, he prepared her to expect to be exposed to brief, repeated memories of The Jump.

As its name implies, EMDR is a technique aimed at aiding the traumatized person to decrease their negative reactions to the event (desensitization) and to change their responses to the trauma (their beliefs, attributions, emotions, etc.) to be more positive and adaptive (reprocessing). The psychologist instructed Abbey to follow his moving finger with her eyes back and forth in quick succession. While doing this, she was to recall The Jump in as much vividness and detail as possible. These eye movements are used as dual attention stimuli—something to focus Abbey's attention on an external stimulus while she is reprocessing her internalized trauma. These reprocessing episodes were intense but very brief. Although eye movements are featured in the name of this technique, other dual attention stimuli, such as finger taps to the person's hand, sounds, lights, and others, have been employed. After these reprocessing exercises, Abbey was asked to describe her feelings, attitudes, memories, and anything else that occurred to her. These were noted and interpreted. Finally, she found more positive ways to reprocess The Jump, such as realizing that she couldn't have possibly helped the jumper, that the attack resulted from complex geopolitical issues and had nothing to do with her own characteristics or failings, that surviving or perishing in the attack was a matter of luck and placement and not a reflection of personal worth, and so on.

After three EMDR sessions, she noted that her PTSD symptoms had reduced significantly; she now felt ready to go back to work. After eight sessions she felt comfortable terminating individual therapy.

PROGNOSIS

Abbey's symptoms had been reduced significantly. For the most part her dreams and flashbacks had stopped, and she no longer avoided situations where she might be reminded of her trauma. She became much more interested in social activities: she was seeing her friends regularly and had begun dating. When she returned to work, she didn't want to go back to New York, or even Chicago—although she felt confident that she could have. She had done a good deal of reflecting during her leave, and she decided to apply for jobs in Nashville. She felt a heightened need to balance her interpersonal and emotional needs with her career ambitions. Her parents had a son who was always a half world away and all but impossible to reach; they were thrilled with her decision to return to her hometown. This is not to say that Abbey had forgotten 9-11 or The

Jump. She will always remember that day. But those memories no longer intruded on her day-to-day activities. It was an amazing relief.

Generally PTSD victims respond well to the kind of multi-component treatment that Abbey received. According to figures in the *DSM-IV-TR*, about half recover fully within three months, whereas the other half may show gradually decreasing, waxing and waning, or chronic symptoms. Who develops PTSD also varies quite a bit. Given similar severe traumas, roughly one-third of the victims will develop PTSD symptoms. The factors that best predict who will develop PTSD involve the nature of the trauma: its duration, immediacy, and severity.

CLEANLINESS IS NEXT TO GODLINESS

Perhaps the most famous person to suffer from Obsessive Compulsive Disorder was Howard Hughes, billionaire businessman, pilot, and movie producer. What started off as a minor concern of germs slowly escalated over the years. His anxieties about the cleanliness of food, for example, included worrying about how hygienically it is prepared and how well the dishes, utensils, and glassware is washed. Correspondingly, his eating habits became more and more restrictive, first avoiding restaurants, then only eating prepackaged meals ("TV dinners"), to finally refusing to leave his bed to eat. Toward the end of his life, his illness had become so debilitating that he was unable to leave his own bed—soiling his room and himself with discarded food, tissues, and his own excrement. How ironic for someone so obsessed with cleanliness! We shall hear more about Mr. Hughes in Chapter 13. The following case describes a woman also obsessed with cleanliness, which also restricted her life immensely.

PRESENTING COMPLAINT

Mary is a 68-year-old married homemaker in a middle-class suburb of Pittsburgh. She and her husband have been married for 46 years and have four children and 10 grandchildren. When she presented to the clinic at the urging of her family and priest, this kind, grandmotherly woman was a wreck. This was the first time she had left her home in over 5 years. She looked haggard and exhausted, and her hands were raw and bleeding from open sores, the inevitable result of washing them six to eight *hours* per day for the past several years. Her anxieties were overwhelming to the point where she was afraid to touch anything at all. She had to be coaxed and reassured by her priest just to sit down in a chair. Mary's anxieties also wrought havoc on her relationships. It has been over three years since she had last touched her husband or anyone in her family. She had not left her home for over five years. How did this loving, pious woman get to the state where she avoided her community, her church, and even her family?

Throughout her life Mary has been neat and orderly. She had always had a disdain for dirt and clutter, and she put great effort into keeping her house clean and tidy, which was quite a job with three sons. She was also very careful in her personal habits, typically brushing her teeth three or four times and washing her hands six to eight times per day.

Mary has also been very disciplined in her religious practices. She often worried about whether she had accidentally left anything out during confession and whether she had performed various rituals correctly. Over the past several years, however, her religious worries have become much more intense, leading her to perform rituals that occupy several hours every day. Her increased anxiety seems to focus primarily on one issue: the taking of the wafer during holy communion.

According to traditional Catholic doctrine, the wafer and wine used in the communion ritual are actually part of the Host and are themselves holy. As a result, only someone who is absolved of sin can touch the sacramental elements without contaminating them, and in most churches only priests were allowed to actually touch the wafers. Then in 1969, Pope Paul VI declared that this procedure was no longer necessary. This pronouncement caused great anxiety for many older, traditional Catholics; it was particularly distressing for Mary with her heightened fears of dirt, who dreaded contaminating the Host by touching the wafer.

About 10 years ago her priest retired and was replaced by a younger man who encouraged his parishioners to take their wafers directly. Mary, along with a few others, insisted that he continue to feed her the wafer, and he honored her request. However, Mary's husband, children, and friends now took their wafers directly. Interestingly, Mary did not see her family members as contaminating the Host; rather, their contact with the Holy Spirit allowed the Host to be transferred to everything they touched. This idea began with their drive home from mass. The steering wheel, the door handles, and eventually the entire car was now holy and could not be contaminated by her "impure" touch. Any object at home, be it a chair, a table, the kitchen sink, and even the toilet, was imbued with the Holy Spirit and had to be avoided. In a very literal sense, for Mary the Holy Spirit was everywhere.

Eventually the extreme anxiety generated by this situation became too much to bear, and Mary settled on a compromise that entailed two types of responses. One response was to make herself as clean as possible before she touched anything. Her handwashing became more and more frequent. The other response was to try to rid an object of the Host before she might contaminate it. So she washed everything. Mary's washing compulsions gradually escalated to the point where she would spend hours busily scrubbing fixtures that were already gleaming and wiping furniture that had no visible signs of dust. Perhaps the most tragic aspect of Mary's illness concerned her relationship with her family. She felt she had to limit her contact with her loved ones, and she also insisted that they constantly wash their hands and take frequent showers. Not surprisingly, they responded with annoyance and resentment, and gradually she drifted farther and farther from the family contact that was once so important to her. Mary was well aware of the illogical nature of her thoughts and behaviors, but out of embarrassment she kept her religious anxieties to herself. Along with these anxieties, Mary suffered from intermittent periods of depression, frustration, and hopelessness. Mary had always been in fairly good health, which was fortunate given her wariness of doctors. But ironically it is exactly because she never sought medical treatment that her raw hands and depressed affect went undiagnosed and untreated for so long. Eventually her anxieties and depression became overwhelming, and Mary began to have persistent suicidal thoughts, which themselves were the height of sinfulness. Finally she confided in her husband. After hearing her concerns over contaminating the Holy Spirit, he urged her to discuss this problem with their priest. It was he who finally convinced Mary to seek help at a clinic.

PERSONAL HISTORY

Mary's childhood appears to be unremarkable. She is the second of five children, with an older brother, two younger brothers, and a younger sister. Although Mary described her upbringing as strict, she denies any cruelty or abuse, nor could she think of any particularly upsetting event in her childhood or adolescence.

Mary has a long history of mild obsessions and rituals. For example, she frequently had notions that some numbers were good and others were bad, which would lead her to perform minor compulsions such as buying a certain number of items at a store or inviting a certain number of guests to a party. Mary also admits to having several minor phobias, including spiders, snakes, and some bugs. Mary's problems with her anxieties have waxed and waned over the course of her lifetime, but generally these have not interfered with her duties as wife and mother.

Mary's family history shows no evidence of any mental illness. Mary's daughter, however, has been in therapy for depression and continues to take antidepressant medication. In addition, Mary's oldest son has intermittently suffered from periods of anxiety. From Mary's description, he seems to suffer from panic attacks, but because he has never sought treatment, no diagnosis of panic disorder can be confirmed.

CONCEPTUALIZATION AND TREATMENT

DSM-IV-TR defines obsessive-compulsive disorder (OCD) as the existence of recurrent obsessions or compulsions (or both) of such severity that they cause distress or interfere with everyday activities and relationships.

Obsessions are unwanted, intrusive thoughts, ideas, or impulses that are seen as intrusive and inappropriate. Initially the person tries to ignore the obsession or mask it with some other thought, but the obsession persists. Obsessions take many forms; some of the more common obsessions are contamination (fearing dirt, germs, infection), security (checking that doors are locked or stoves are turned off), doubt (wondering if one has completed simple tasks or has violated a law), illness (fearing that one will become ill), asymmetry (needing to enter doors at the exact middle), saving/hoarding (fearing that items can't be thrown out), violence (worrying about harming a spouse or killing a child), and promiscuity (fearing a loss of control over sexual behavior). The majority suffer from multiple obsessions. Obsessions are almost always greatly anxiety-provoking, both because of their inherently upsetting nature and because in most cases they lead more or less directly to specific compulsions. The person understands that the obsessive thoughts are illogical but nevertheless feels unable to control them.

Compulsions are ritualized, repetitive behaviors performed to reduce anxiety, often the anxiety generated by obsessions. Sometimes, though, compulsions are performed in a stereotyped way or simply because the person somehow feels that the behavior must be performed. The most common compulsions correspond to the common obsessions: checking, washing, counting, asking advice and/or confessing, needing symmetry and precision, repeating, counting, and hoarding. About half of those who suffer from OCD have multiple compulsions. Not all compulsions are expressed in observable behavior, though. Some people engage in covert rituals, such as silently reciting stereotyped statements or counting to themselves. Covert compulsions are harder to recognize, but once they are identified they can be treated in the same manner as overt rituals.

Most people are greatly distressed by their compulsive behavior, recognizing that the compulsive behavior is excessive and disruptive and serves little practical function. Usually the person attempts to resist the compulsion, at least initially, but anxiety increases to the point where the compulsion must be performed. People with OCD do not enjoy the compulsive behavior. Behavior patterns that are initially enjoyable but become uncontrollable, such as compulsive gambling, are not true compulsions and are probably better thought of as addictions.

Mary's deep-seated and persistent fear of contaminating the Holy Spirit followed the pattern of a classic contamination obsession, but with one unusual twist: Mary wasn't afraid of being contaminated; instead, she was afraid of being the contaminating agent through her own impure nature. This obsession led her to perform the typical washing compulsions of excessive handwashing and persistent washing and wiping of everything (and everyone) in her home.

Goodman and his associates (Goodman, Price, Rasmussen, Mazure, Fleischmann, et al., 1989; Goodman, Price, Rasmussen, Mazure, Delgado, et al., 1989) developed the Yale-Brown Obsessive-Compulsive Scale (Y-BOCS), which provides an objective measure of the severity of obsessions and compulsions. The Y-BOCS is administered by the therapist and consists of 10 questions, 5 concerning the severity of obsessions and 5 concerning the severity of compulsions. The therapist scores each item from 0 (no pathology) to 4 (extreme pathology). Thus, total scores can range from 0 to 40.

During Mary's initial interview she scored a 32 on the Y-BOCS, indicating severe to extreme problems with virtually every aspect of her obsessions and compulsions. Of more immediate concern, however, was Mary's severe depression, as indicated by her depressed mood, lethargy, and suicidal ideas. Her score of 34 on the Hamilton Rating Scale for Depression (HRSD) (Hamilton, 1967) indicated severely depressed mood. Because Mary had no history of previous depressed episodes, and because her depression appeared to result from her inability to control her compulsions and from her consequent estrangement from her family, her therapist concluded that her depression was most likely secondary to her OCD.

The majority of OCD patients are treated on a five- to eight-week outpatient treatment program. Mary's treatment started with medication. Most physicians begin with an SSRI antidepressant such as Zoloft or Celexa, which is effective for both the depressive and anxious symptoms. Once her depression was beginning to respond, behavior therapy began. Behavior therapy for OCD consists of two elements: exposure therapy and behavioral contracting.

As the name suggests, exposure therapy calls for patients to be exposed to the objects of the obsessions that are feared, and then prevented from performing the compulsion that typically relieves their fears. Gradually the patient's anxiety will begin to decrease without resorting to the compulsion, and through extinction the connection between the obsession and the compulsion will be weakened and eventually broken.

In Mary's case the object of the obsession was the Holy Spirit, so her therapist arranged to work with her priest, who was very cooperative. Because Mary's obsessions began with the holy wafer, this was used in her therapy. At first the priest handled a wafer and then placed his hands on the kitchen table. She was not allowed to wash the table beforehand, nor was she allowed to wipe it afterward. Mary was able to tolerate this situation surprisingly easily, perhaps because of her medication. As she became accustomed to having an "unclean" table, the therapist then had Mary touch the table herself. Again, Mary was not allowed to wash her hands or the table. At first Mary showed moderate levels of anxiety to this procedure, but gradually her fears subsided. Finally Mary was asked to hold a wafer herself. After a few sessions she was able to do this with little anxiety, and the exposure portion of her treatment was considered complete.

The second stage of Mary's behavior therapy was behavior contracting. Mary was instructed to make specific agreements that would limit her compulsive behavior. These contracts were to be in writing and signed by Mary, her husband, and her therapist. One of her initial contracts was that she would wash her hands no more than 10 times a day. Soon this agreement was amended to allow only five daily handwashings. Generally these behavior contracts provide the patient with a formal way to resist the need to perform compulsions and with support from others to aid in this resistance.

After eight weekly sessions of behavior therapy, Mary's obsessive thoughts and compulsive behaviors were reduced dramatically. She washed her hands fewer than five times a day, and she made no attempt to clean objects around the home in any excessive way. Most importantly, she no longer felt the need to avoid her family members. Her scores on both the Y-BOCS and the HRSD were 9, showing mild levels of disturbance on both measures. Her medication dose was reduced to a maintenance level, and her therapy was reduced to checkup sessions every 90 days.

PROGNOSIS

Mary was seen for follow-up one year after treatment. She still reported mild obsessive thinking, but she felt relatively little disturbance from her obsessive thoughts and a virtual absence of compulsive behavior. Mary was most pleased with her relationships with her family, which she described as close and sup-portive. A follow-up session one year later revealed no substantial changes in the intervening year. At both her one-year and her two-year follow-up sessions, she scored below 10 on the Y-BOCS and the HRSD.

Mary died of a massive heart attack about five years later. Her husband reported that she continued to have mild obsessive thoughts, mostly related to doubt concerning her participation in religious rituals. However, these were never really disruptive. He could not think of a clear instance of a compulsion in the past few years.

ALTERED STATES

PRESENTING COMPLAINT

Sherry is a 48-year-old nurse's aid who has received inpatient psychiatric care off and on for the past five years. Approximately two weeks after her most recent readmission, she became very confused about her surroundings and complained that "everything had changed." She demanded to know who had rearranged the hospital and the grounds, and she repeatedly asked to see people who didn't exist, both patients and staff members. When staff members attempted to calm her, she became verbally and physically abusive, shouting obscenities and swinging her fists.

Sherry had been admitted with a diagnosis of schizophrenia, disorganized type. She had a history of previous hospitalizations, and her strange and irrational behavior seemed to be clear evidence of yet another psychotic episode. A new psychologist on staff, however, believed that Sherry's behavior might be evidence of a dissociative state, a state of consciousness where one part of her awareness is split off from another. Sherry was given the Hypnotic Induction Profile (HIP) and was found to be highly hypnotizable, scoring a 4 out of a possible 5. While in a hypnotic trance, she gave the present date as being eight months earlier than it in fact was and stated that she was at a hospital over a thousand miles away. The date she gave and her description of the hospital corresponded to a clinic she attended just prior to her most recent admission. The therapist who hypnotized her found that she had no memory of anything after leaving this clinic; it was as if she had lost the last eight months of her life. Through hypnosis, Sherry was able to experience age regression (a reliving of the past as though it were the present) to the time of her earlier hospitalization. After the session involving age regression, she was able to reorient herself to her present time and location, and her apparently psychotic behavior diminished.

Amnesic periods were not new to Sherry; she experienced many episodes for which she had no memory. Sherry is a quiet, demure, and conscientious person, but her behavior often changes during her amnesic episodes. According to the reports of her friends, family, and past therapists, her behavior during these blackouts was often hostile, angry, and self-destructive. Although Sherry could not remember what she did during these episodes, she would often find physical evidence of her odd behavior. Sometimes she would notice new cuts and bruises on her body, and on several occasions she woke up to find herself in bed with a strange man after having had unprotected sex. For Sherry, the knowledge that she could not control her own behavior was positively frightening.

A recent blackout period occurred about three weeks ago. Under hypnosis Sherry experienced age regression back three weeks to the time of this amnesic episode. After a minute or so, she suddenly looked up at the psychologist and sneered, "What the hell do you want?" Her voice and tone had changed completely from the shy woman who had gone into the hypnotic trance; she was now hostile, angry, and sarcastic. The therapist was somewhat startled by Sherry's sudden change in tone, but he remained calm and asked Sherry who she was. She responded, "Why should I answer you; I don't owe you anything!" When the psychologist asked her if she were Sherry, she snapped, "Hell, no! Not that mouse. I'm Karla."

The therapist then asked "Karla" what had happened just now (that is, during the amnesic episode Sherry experienced three weeks ago). Karla made it clear that she was irritated at the intrusion on her time and gruffly explained what happened. She had just picked up a man at a bar with the intention of going back to his apartment. But Sherry had spoiled her fun by crying at the bar, causing the man to lose interest. Determined to punish Sherry, Karla threatened to inflict a deep cut on Sherry's leg. With intense hatred and bitterness, Karla ran an imaginary knife over a recently healed cut on her leg, shouting, "I'll show her; I'll really cut her this time! I'll go to sleep and let her find it!" She then closed her eyes. When her eyes reopened, her voice and manner were those of Sherry. Sherry gently touched the wound and sobbed quietly. When the

42

therapist asked her how she got this cut, she appeared to be confused and hesitantly replied, "Well, I . . . I don't know. I guess I ran into something."

PERSONAL HISTORY

Sherry has a twin sister. They both had suffered numerous episodes of physical abuse and neglect throughout their childhoods. At one time their mother bloodied Sherry's nose, and on another occasion she broke Sherry's tooth with her fist. Both of these events occurred before the age of 4. Once Sherry's mother also threw a pot of boiling water at her in a fit of rage, leaving her with second-degree burns on her arms and chest. Sherry's parents divorced after a bitter marriage lasting five years. Two years later her mother remarried. Unfortunately for the twins, their new stepfather was also violent; as his primary form of punishment he would beat the twins using a board studded with nails. After three or four years Sherry and her sister moved in with their biological father. Although he was more caring than the mother and stepfather, he nevertheless was capable of abuse, particularly during his frequent alcoholic binges. On these occasions he would beat the twin girls with a belt buckle. After several years Sherry's mother obtained a court order that gave her custody of the children. Immediately after winning their custody, however, the mother sent the twins off to live at a strict boarding school. Sherry's mediocre grades precluded any realistic chance of being admitted to a good college, so after graduation she joined the Army and was separated from her sister for the first time.

For most of her life, Sherry dealt with the anxiety of this abuse and neglect by dissociating the traumas onto her sister. That is, she frequently experienced her physical and psychological pain as having happened to her twin sister instead of to herself. For example, Sherry stated that her mother once threw boiling water at her sister. However, her mother's and sister's testimony (the mother describing an "accident"), as well as her medical records, show that in actuality Sherry was the one who was scalded as a child. It was not until she was separated from her sister, however, that she began to experience uncontrollable amnesic periods.

When Sherry joined the Army, she had hopes of being trained as a nurse, but her Army career had barely begun when trouble arose. During basic training she began to notice long periods of time that she could not remember. Her behavior during these periods was reported to be wild and unpredictable; she would often begin violent arguments with other recruits, and on several occasions she had sexual relations with male soldiers on the base or with strange men she would pick up at the local bars. Sherry had no recollection of these actions, and at the time suspected that she was being singled out unfairly, though she was never able to provide an alibi due to her frequent blackouts. She also made several suicidal gestures during her amnesic episodes, usually in the form of cutting herself on the forearms and/or taking overdoses of tranquilizers. In addition, she had gone to the camp infirmary on several occasions and complained of auditory hallucinations and depression. As a result of her bizarre and disruptive behavior, Sherry received a psychiatric discharge and was hospitalized with a diagnosis of schizophrenia, disorganized type. While in the hospital she was given chlorpromazine (Thorazine), an antipsychotic medication, which did little to relieve her symptoms.

Over the next fifteen years Sherry was admitted to several different psychiatric institutions under different diagnoses, including bipolar disorder, major depression, schizophrenia, and borderline personality disorder. As a result she has been treated with lithium and a variety of antidepressant and antipsychotic medications. All of these efforts, however, had little lasting effect.

CONCEPTUALIZATION AND TREATMENT

Three aspects of Sherry's history were fundamental in the conceptualization of her case. First, Sherry has a strong dissociative capacity, as evidenced by her high hypnotizability and her frequent amnesic periods. Second, she suffered relatively severe and persistent abuse and neglect as a child. Third, and most crucial, consciousness was split between two very different personalities. These characteristics are the hallmarks of someone suffering from dissociative identity disorder (DID), formerly called multiple personality disorder.

People with strong dissociative capacities, even those who have suffered significant childhood traumas, do not necessarily develop multiple personalities. Generally they will utilize their dissociation skill as a defense against particularly painful experiences, a sort of emotional buffer, simply by "zoning out," that is, becoming psychologically unaware of the abuse they are suffering. They experience this as an amnesic episode. In some cases, however, the dissociation process itself becomes involuntary and uncontrollable. Frequent blackout periods and reports of uncharacteristic behavior are indications of these involuntary dissociations. Finding themselves unable to control their behavior, these people are then compelled (either by their own fears or by the insistence of others) to seek psychological help. This seems to be the case with Sherry. Based on this conceptualization, the psychologist established a diagnosis of DID with histrionic, psychotic, and depressive features. He recommended to the medical staff that they discontinue her antipsychotic medication, which in any event did not seem to be effective.

Sherry's therapy was organized into five stages. The first was aimed at recognizing and eventually controlling her dissociations. Using Sherry's hypnotizability as a therapeutic tool, the therapist attempted to provide structure to her spontaneous dissociative states through formal hypnosis. The therapist regularly contacted Karla during hypnotic trances. As therapy progressed, Sherry was gradually trained in self-hypnosis techniques, which gave her a measure of control over her dissociative states.

The second stage of psychotherapy involved setting limits on her self-destructive tendencies. Using self-hypnosis and cognitive therapy, she was taught to re-experience her past psychological traumas and was urged to not blame herself for her past abuse. Sherry was also taught to express her emotions more openly in an attempt to develop an outlet for her hostility other than Karla. On a more behavioral level, Sherry was frequently hospitalized for short periods to prevent her from carrying out her suicidal threats. In addition, fluoxetine (Prozac), an SSRI antidepressant, was administered to counteract her depressive symptoms.

The third stage of therapy focused on the relationship between the patient and the therapist. Given Sherry's history of almost continuous abuse and neglect, one would expect significant trust issues. Indeed, initially she suspected that the therapist was interested in her only because she was a fascinating case that would lend him prestige if he could cure her. In this light her frequent suicidal gestures were seen as tests of his commitment. Would he remain concerned for her welfare even at the risk of professional failure? At this stage it was essential for the therapist to face the possibility of failure as well as to convey a genuine interest in her well-being in spite of her suicidal gestures and her resistance to therapy. His job was to be there for her and not to give up, though at the same time setting limits on her.

The fourth, and perhaps the most crucial, stage of therapy involved integrating the two personalities into one being. To accomplish this, Sherry first had to be convinced that the hostile and disruptive aspects of her subconscious were valuable and should not be suppressed. Indeed, the assertiveness and self-confidence expressed by Karla were assets that should be incorporated into a more well-rounded personality. One technique that promoted this integration was giving "equal time" to both "Sherry" and "Karla." In this way, Sherry learned to tolerate Karla's more aggressive emotions, thus reducing the need for Karla to rebel and undermine Sherry. Similarly, Karla was taught that Sherry's good-natured attributes could be quite useful in forming and maintaining relationships with others. Over a period of two years, both personalities gradually incorporated elements of the other, and the shifts between them became smoother and less disruptive. Now Sherry reported that she was aware of Karla for the first time. She described this realization as "opening a door in myself."

Another important aspect of this integration was to have the patient understand the traumatic memories and events that caused the dissociations in the first place. However, the therapist must be cautious in this endeavor. On the one hand, rushing a patient to relive early traumas too quickly can exacerbate the dissociations. On the other hand, failing to deal with repressed traumas may perpetuate the need for dissociations in the future. In general, these patients are encouraged to confront and accept their painful memories, to gain control over these memories, and to restructure these memories in a way that is consistent with their emerging unified self-image.

In Sherry's case, her mother's persistent manipulation and neglect engendered extreme emotional dependence, which led to persistent feelings of guilt and obligation. Understandably, Sherry was very resentful of her mother's callous selfishness, yet she felt unable to challenge her directly. Instead she would criticize herself for being so weak and dependent. Often this self-derogation and repressed anger was expressed by Karla, who would cut Sherry's wrists or perform other acts of self-mutilation to punish Sherry for being so weak. To prevent Sherry from venting her frustration in self-destructive ways in the future, her psychologist urged her to confront her mother. This was not without some cost; Sherry entered a severe depression after this episode. However, she responded well to antidepressant medication and began to function better after her recovery.

Finally, the fifth stage of Sherry's therapy involved interaction management. This is a therapy technique used to teach the patient more effective ways of dealing with other people through the use of role-playing and modeling. As a part of this therapy, Sherry attended conjoint sessions with her mother, her sister, and, later, her boyfriend. The therapist then provided Sherry with ways to be more assertive when reacting to the various interpersonal demands of these people.

The course of Sherry's therapy was very gradual. After her discharge from the hospital, she attended weekly psychotherapy on an outpatient basis. After three years both personalities had finally recognized each other, and shortly thereafter she began a relationship with a man. Her outpatient therapy, which took the form of frequent office consultations and occasional active interventions, continued for two more years. During this time Sherry broke up with her boyfriend and entered a severe depressive episode. However, she made no serious suicide attempts and was able to remain an outpatient. Her outpatient therapy drew to a close about one year later. Approximately three years later Sherry was raped. At that time she was brought to the hospital in a confused and agitated state. Hypnotic regression enabled her to relive the painful events of the rape and to convince herself that she was not responsible for the trauma. She was released from the hospital after two days. For the past few years Sherry has received supportive psychotherapy off and on at her own request.

PROGNOSIS

Sherry has made steady progress since the beginning of therapy. Over the course of several years, her uncontrolled bursts of anger and self-mutilating behaviors for the most part have ceased, she has developed a more equitable relationship with her mother, and her therapy has generally progressed. However, she remains vulnerable to future dissociative episodes in response to severe stress, particularly if it involves sexual or financial exploitation.

Sherry's power to dissociate is a two-edged sword. On the one hand, her ability to repress the traumatic events of her life might serve to insulate her from severely painful experiences. But on the other hand, this ability can also leave her open to uncontrollable dissociations. Sherry's continued adjustment will depend on her ability to learn to use her powers of self-hypnosis to gain mastery over her dissociation. The prognosis for Sherry is generally guarded; she has improved significantly, but she remains vulnerable to future traumas. Perhaps her most difficult test will be when her mother dies. Although it may seem that she would feel a measure of relief at the passing of this abusive and callous mother, the mother's very controlling nature made Sherry very dependent, and a separation by death will be very difficult.

BIG WOMAN ON CAMPUS

PRESENTING COMPLAINT

Julie is a 20-year-old sophomore at a small Midwestern college. For the last five days she has gone without any sleep whatsoever and has gone "super-hyper." She has been caught up in a lot of exciting ideas that came so fast she could barely keep them straight. Everyone else seemed to have a hard time keeping up with her pace too, and they kept asking her to slow down. Her thoughts were new and exciting, and they seemed so logical and right. These ideas often took on a mystical or sexual tone, or they involved her developing her political power. But everyone else either couldn't understand what she was saying, or they thought she was just weird. Well, their loss. She couldn't slow down for these losers; she was riding a real high.

For one thing, she proclaimed to a group of friends that she did not menstruate because she was "of a third sex, a gender above the two human sexes." When they asked her what she meant, she explained that she is a "superwoman" who can avoid human sexuality and still give birth. Another line of thought involved global disarmament. She felt that she had somehow switched souls with the senior senator from her state. From his thoughts and memories, she developed six theories of government that would allow her to save the world from nuclear destruction. She proclaimed these six theories to friends and even to professors, and she began to campaign for election to the U.S. Senate. She felt it was kind of a re-election, since his thoughts were really hers now anyway.

Julie was worried that she would forget some of her thoughts, so she began writing these thoughts everywhere: in her notebooks, on her personal computer, and even on the walls of her dormitory room. Julie's friends were shocked to find her room in total disarray, with hundreds of frantic and often incoherent messages written all over the walls and furniture.

By the end of the week Julie was beginning to feel increasingly irritated and fatigued. She complained of her leg being numb, although she seemed to walk on it just fine. She had neglected her classes and was obnoxious to her friends, which was not like her at all. Her high finally ended when she was found by campus police naked on the lawn in front of the student health service.

As she sat in the exam room, she was confused and groggy. She still spoke very rapidly, but now in a rambling, loose manner. The physician on staff hospitalized her, and the psychiatric resident on call prescribed haloperidol (Haldol), an antipsychotic medication. Over the next few days, Julie's delusions (systems of thought based on false or bizarre foundations) gradually receded. When she woke up the next morning, a psychiatrist interviewed her:

Therapist: Julie, do you know where you are?

Julie: I don't know. It's a hospital room.

Therapist: Well, why are you here?

Julie: I have a lot of trouble walking and I need to walk because I have so many things to do before the election like make up posters, TV spots, interviews, and all that stuff.

Therapist: What did you say about your leg? You said something's wrong with it, didn't you?

Julie: Oh, yeah. Well, sometimes I can't feel it because it's really another person's leg and I can't always control it.

Therapist: You just said that your leg is really another person's leg. It that right?

Julie: I did? You know, this has happened to me before, the leg thing, I mean. And being confused. I had to go to the hospital then, too.

Previous Episodes

In the course of therapy, Julie described two earlier episodes of manic, bizarre behavior. These episodes were both followed by periods of intense depression.

Julie's first manic episode occurred during high school. She was 17 in the summer between her junior and senior years, Julie went to a tennis summer camp with several other boys and girls her own age. During the trip she began to develop a strong attraction toward one of the boys. She had never had these feelings before, and they frightened her. She became extremely self-conscious about her sexual thoughts, and she became convinced that everyone else was constantly watching her and could read her mind. Although she never developed a relationship with the boy, she felt that she could not stand to be so near to him and had to leave. She returned home after one week. She felt "safe" at home, and her agitation quickly subsided. She did not date during the remainder of the summer or during her senior year which passed with no further incidents.

Julie, now 18, then went off to a private university in the East. After being away at college for 10 days, she developed a severe depression. She could not bring herself to attend classes or any campus activities. She suffered from a number of somatic difficulties characteristic of depression, including poor appetite, insomnia, an inability to concentrate, and psychomotor retardation. After two weeks Julie left school and was admitted to a psychiatric hospital near her parents' home. While in the hospital she was given Haldol, like now. She also attended group sessions and individual therapy. Gradually her depressed symptoms dissipated, and she was discharged after seven days. She followed up with weekly appointments with a psychologist while she stayed home for the rest of the semester.

At the beginning of the next semester, Julie enrolled in a private university in the Midwest. Her past anxious and depressed episodes last semester and in high school made her feel as though she had missed many social opportunities commonly experienced by other 19-year-olds, and she decided to make a change this time and to have a "real college experience." Julie made friends with a group of students who smoked, drank, did a variety of recreational drugs, and engaged in casual sex, including group masturbation, lesbian encounters, and unprotected intercourse. Over the next several weeks she became increasingly irritable and restless, and she had difficulty sleeping and concentrating. Her use of marijuana and ecstasy increased, as did her reckless behavior. Once she woke up in the lounge of a fraternity wearing only a sheet, without any memory of what she might have done the night before.

As the semester wore on, she became increasingly erratic. She developed clearly bizarre thoughts and behaviors that revolved around themes of responsibility, sexuality, and religion. She often felt as if she could control the world; at times she felt that she could prevent nuclear war, and at other times she felt personally responsible for nuclear explosions that she believed she felt through slight ground tremors. She also suffered from what she described as a "Jesus Christ delirium." She felt a special empathy with Christ, and she experienced vivid episodes where Christ talked directly to her. She wanted to "merge with the higher spirits," and at times she felt her body "floating up to heaven." Her delusions often included ideas about the special significance of parts of her body. For example, she felt that the follicles on the left side of her head were sensitized to receive thought messages from Christ. Many times she also attempted to include other people in these delusions. Once her boyfriend came into her room and saw her caressing her own breasts and thighs. When he teased her about how sexy she looked, she became very offended and insisted that her right leg and hand were actually his, and thus it was he who was really stroking her body by controlling them.

As she gradually lost control over her psychotic behaviors, she began to get the attention of university officials. Several students complained to her resident assistant after they watched her repeatedly chanting "work . . . work . . . work." Finally she was hospitalized after she began babbling about finding the biblical garden during a lecture she was attending. At first she only muttered to herself, but eventually her incoherent babbling became audible to the entire class. Suddenly she ran out of the classroom, and security officers found her wandering around the campus.

Julie was admitted to the university hospital, where she was again put on Haldol, but this time she was also given lithium, a mood stabilizer. She was again enrolled in group and individual therapy, where she developed a good relationship with her psycho-therapist. After two weeks of intensive group and individual thera-py, her bizarre ideation gradually diminished, and she was released and returned to school. Although she was told to continue taking lithium, she complained of the nausea and diarrhea it caused and soon discontinued taking it.

Approximately a month after leaving the hospital, Julie began to feel depressed. Again, she experienced difficulty with eating, sleeping, and concentrating. She discontinued her favorite pastime, painting, and stopped going to classes. Finally, she withdrew from the university and returned home to the Midwest. She was not treated for her depression, which gradually lifted during the summer. At the insistence of her parents, Julie then enrolled in a small college near her home.

PERSONAL HISTORY

Julie grew up in what she termed was a traditional Irish-Catholic home, by which she meant she had overprotective and demanding parents. Of the five children, she was the one who always obeyed her parents and played the role of the good girl of the family, a role she describes as being "the Little Miss Perfect." Julie described herself as being quite dependent on her parents, who treated her as if she were a much younger child. In contrast to her passive obedience, Julie describes her siblings as rebellious. Her older brother openly defied the Catholic church by announcing his atheism, and her older sister had made it known to her parents that she was sexually active while she was still in high school. Julie also describes her two younger sisters as defiant, but to a lesser extent.

Julie describes her parents as exceptionally strict with respect to sexual matters; they never discussed issues related to sex except to make it clear that their children are to remain virgins until they are married. Throughout high school her mother forbade her to wear makeup. She detested wearing dresses because they somehow made her feel a lack of control. She remembers being shocked and frightened when she began menstruating; she was especially distressed at the loss of control this entailed. Julie did not date during high school, and until recently has not had a steady boyfriend in college.

Julie's family history shows evidence of mood disorders: her maternal grandfather received electroconvulsive therapy (ECT) for depression, and her father's aunt was diagnosed with a "nervous breakdown," which apparently was a depressive episode at meno-pause. Julie believes that her father has been depressed for years, although he has never sought professional treatment.

CONCEPTUALIZATION AND TREATMENT

Julie suffers from episodes of wild and reckless manic behavior alternating with episodes of moderate to severe depression. This pattern is a prime indication of manic-depressive illness, which *DSM-IV-TR* terms Bipolar I Disorder. (Bipolar II Disorder involves episodes of depression and hypomania, a more mild elevation of mood and behavior which never gets as out of control as a full-blown mania.) To many therapists her grandiose and bizarre delusions would be taken as signs of a psychotic disorder like schizophrenia. However, her history of alternating manic and depressed episodes and the fact that her psychotic symptoms seemed to correspond to her disordered mood (that is, the delusions that appear during her manic episodes are primarily grandiose and/or expansive; those that manifest during the depressed episodes are critical and judgmental) point toward a diagnosis of Bipolar I Disorder with psychotic features, or, to use an obsolete, less formal term, manic-depressive psychosis.

The initial consideration of Julie's psychiatrist is to control her florid psychotic symptoms. Her initial treatment consisted of antipsychotic medication in a controlled hospital environment. Once Julie's therapist became aware of her history of past manic and depressed episodes, he prescribed lithium carbonate along with Haldol to reduce her wild mood swings. Once the bizarre psychotic features abate, Julie will gradually be taken off halperodol. However, she will most likely remain on lithium or some other mood stabilizer for the rest of her life. Julie's therapist maintains her lithium level at approximately 0.5 milliequivalent per liter of blood, confirmed by biweekly blood tests. For Julie, this amounts to a dose of 1200 milligrams per day.

In addition to medication, psychotherapy was performed, with the goal of having Julie increase her self-acceptance and to teach her ways to assert her autonomy and independence in appropriate, beneficial ways. In Julie's case, her experimentation with drugs and sex was an attempt to change her self-image, but these experiences created conflicts that she could not cope with. Still, Julie still has a need to free herself of at least some of the strict constraints imposed by her parents and her faith. With this in mind, Julie's therapist had her engage in a "mini-rebellion." After her hospitalization, Julie had to decide whether to stay at home for a while or to return to school. She was encouraged to return to school as a way of developing a sense of separation from her parents. This she did. Julie was also told to think about the conflict between her wants and her duties and how she might resolve these problems. A question Julie was told to keep in her mind was, "When is Little Miss Perfect right, and when is she wrong?"

In addition to her individual therapy, Julie was also involved in a depression therapy group. Julie found the supportive atmosphere of the group to be extremely helpful in letting her overcome her shyness about telling people about her illness. Because Julie was the only student in the group with Bipolar Disorder and had by far the most unusual experiences, the other group members treated her with respect and a certain degree of celebrity. Julie told her therapist that it felt good being able to help other people just by being open and friendly.

The focus of therapy then shifted to altering Julie's impressions of the demands of her parents and the church. For this the therapist employed a process of cognitive restructuring. One issue involved Julie's perception of sex. In therapy Julie frequently admonished herself for having sexual fantasies and for her past promiscuity. The therapist emphasized that sexual feelings are common to everyone, particularly young people her age, and that having sexual feelings was not something to be ashamed of or afraid of. A second issue was Julie's dependence on her parents' approval. Julie often refrained from doing something she would have enjoyed for fear that her parents, especially her mother, might disapprove. It was emphasized that Julie should not deny her mother's values; rather she was encouraged to accept them for what they are: another person's ideas that may be different from her own.

The final stage of Julie's therapy involved support and maintenance. Julie's weekly visits now dealt primarily with supporting her sense of autonomy from her parents, especially in the areas in which they disagree. Just as important as her psychological support, these visits helped her maintain a proper level of lithium in her system. Every other week she has the lithium level of her blood analyzed to ensure that she maintains an effective yet safe lithium blood level.

PROGNOSIS

As is the case with the many patients with Bipolar I Disorder, Julie responded well to treatment with a mood stabilizer. As of 13 months after her most recent manic episode, Julie appears to be doing well. She is still in supportive therapy, which has now been reduced to a monthly basis. Julie is still somewhat tense and anxious, but she has had no psychotic symptoms since her last episode. Julie is very bright (so far she has earned a 3.6 GPA in college in spite of the disruptions caused by her illness) and has a great deal of insight into the causes of her problems. She describes her boyfriend as supportive and undemanding, and her relationship with him seems to be going well. One concern for the future is the eventual possibility of a future pregnancy. Lithium is contraindicated for pregnant women, so she will need to interrupt her lithium therapy if she decides to become pregnant. Julie fears that she might relapse into another manic episode when she discontinues her medication. This is a legitimate concern. Given her past issues with duty and sexuality, this is likely to be a difficult time for her.

The early onset of Julie's disease, the relative frequency of her episodes, and the severity of the psychotic symptoms all indicate that her case of Bipolar I Disorder is quite severe, and it is likely that she will require future hospitalizations at different points in the future, particularly during stressful life events. As a whole, people with bipolar illness tend to be more fragile psychologically. For example, the suicide rate among bipolars is twice that of those who suffer unipolar depression. A further problem is the treatment itself; lithium carbonate is a strong psychoactive agent that has many potentially serious side effects. Gastrointestinal difficulties such as nausea and diarrhea are common. Worse, prolonged elevated levels can result in irreversible kidney and/or thyroid damage. For these reasons treatment with lithium and other mood stabilizers must be closely regulated. Nevertheless, this is not to say that she cannot be productive, successful, and happy. Although Julie has shown that she is prone to manic and depressed episodes, she has also shown that she responds well to lithium and possesses a keen insight into the nature of her disorder. Thus, she has a good chance of seeking appropriate help when needed.

WHO CARES ABOUT OLD CARS?

PRESENTING COMPLAINT

Like many Americans, Jeff has loved cars for as long as he can remember. Throughout his childhood he collected toy cars and built models. As he grew older, his infatuation became a passion. About ten years ago he bought a dilapidated 1956 Chevy Bel Air two-door hardtop. Over the next several years he lovingly restored it to show-winning condition. Last year he bought a Corvette of the same vintage, which though drivable will require significant restoration work in his specially prepared garage workshop. He is a car fanatic outside his garage as well. He watches at least one car race every weekend, subscribes to eleven car magazines, and serves as vice president of the Motor City Chapter of the Tri-Chevy Association. He doesn't mind the winter planning meetings with other club officers, but he lives for the frequent summer events, where he can live and breathe Detroit iron.

This weekend his club met at the Blue Top Drive-In, but he didn't go. In the last two months he had missed three similar events and one planning meeting. His favorite parts stores went unvisited, races went unwatched, magazines piled up unread, his Vette languished untouched. He hadn't even driven his pristine Bel Air for over a month. The cars he had loved so fervently before now held nothing for him. As he said, "My give-a-crap meter is on zero."

Work was pretty much the same story. He used to feel lucky; he designed cars and got paid for it. He even got a promotion a few months ago, from design engineer to project manager. At first things seemed to go well, but soon he started having trouble getting his new staff organized, and they fell behind on their deadlines. The more he was pushed to make his group productive, the more out of control things got. One engineer transferred to another department, and others were looking to leave. Even his secretary was being resentful and defensive. He knew his group was doing badly, but he had no idea what he should do. So he did nothing, and gradually he stopped caring. He called in sick as much as he dared. He wasn't turning out to be such a great manager after all.

Nor was he a great father. It used to be that dinner was always family time, and after dinner he always made time for the girls, bathing them (until they got too old for that), reading them stories, or playing computer games. Only after they were tucked in bed did he retreat to his sacred workshop downstairs. But in the last few months he had barely talked to his children. He cannot remember at what point their games became annoying and irritating, or the point at which he began stare at the TV all evening, not really caring what was on. Eventually he gave up the TV too, because he couldn't stand Renee's accusing looks when she passed by. Now when he came home he just went to the garage and sat.

He stared blankly at his two '56 Chevys. Once they had been his pride and joys. Now when he looked at them he felt nothing. Nothing seemed to matter anymore: his cars, his job, his family. His life? Thoughts about his death occurred frequently in the past few weeks, and they returned now. It was hard to see the point of living. There was his family, but he had life insurance. Would it be enough to support them? Probably. Would Renee remarry? Undoubtedly. And no doubt to a much better husband and father than he was. But a suicide might be hard on Renee and the girls. It would be better if it were an accident. Walk in front of a bus? Crash into a bridge support? He wouldn't use his Chevys, that would be wasteful. The Camaro would do. It used to be that thoughts of his death made him a little scared, but lately they seemed to have a calming effect. As he was sitting there calmly contemplating his suicide, the phone rang.

Jeff: Yeah?

Bill: Hey, Jeff, it's Bill! We missed you this weekend. I haven't seen you in a while.

Jeff: Yeah, well. . .

Bill: How's the Vette coming?

Jeff: About the same; I haven't done much. I haven't done anything. Nothing.

Bill: You know, you don't sound too good. Is everything all right?

Jeff: I don't know.

Bill: You know, Jeff, you sound pretty down. Are you feeling OK? Do you want to talk to somebody or something? Is there anything I can do?

Jeff: I don't know. Maybe there is something.

Bill: Name it.

Jeff: What's the name of your friend in the Psych Department, the one at the clinic?

Five minutes later the phone rang again, and a man introduced himself as "Bill's friend from the clinic." After some brief introductions he asked Jeff to describe what led to his referral for therapy. After Jeff recounted his thoughts that night, the therapist asked Jeff to meet him at the university hospital in twenty minutes. He then asked Jeff to put Renee on the phone. He explained who he was and that Jeff needed to go to the hospital, maybe for a few days. And, he added, *she* was to drive.

PERSONAL HISTORY

Jeff is a 43-year-old mechanical engineer employed as a design manager for an automobile corporation in Detroit. Renee is an assistant principal of an elementary school. They and their two daughters live in an upper-middle-class suburb.

Jeff grew up in a middle-class suburb of Cleveland. His father was the vice president and general manager of a small manufacturing firm until his retirement seven years ago. His mother held a series of part-time secretarial jobs. Jeff has two older sisters. The elder is an oncologist in San Francisco; she is divorced. The younger is married to a real estate broker and does not work outside the home.

Jeff's father ran his company with a firm hand, and he did the same with his family, especially his only son. He rarely gave praise for work well done, though he was quick to criticize any mistake. He made little fuss when Jeff graduated with his master's degree, nor even when Jeff's sister graduated from medical school. Jeff's mother was a relative nonentity in the house who was completely dominated by her overbearing husband. Jeff denied any psychologically traumatic episodes or abuse. His father did use corporal punishment, but Jeff never saw it as excessive or unwarranted. "He'd pop us once in a while, but he never lost control, and we generally knew what we were in for before it happened."

When asked to describe his marriage, at first he could only talk about what a poor father and husband he was, how he found almost everything Renee and the girls did was annoying and point-less. Lately they interacted very little, and when they did they treated him with a mixture of concern, frustration, and contempt. When he was asked to describe some fun family event, his attitude took on a wistful tone, as if he was remembering a pleasant vacation long past.

Jeff has a negative view toward his job as well. Before the past few months, Jeff's generally enjoyed his job. He had the unavoidable conflicts with demanding bosses and disgruntled subordinates, but on the whole he looked forward to work. But things changed after his promotion. The productivity of his group declined rapidly, but the section chief became more insistent that Jeff's group be productive. He felt trapped and overwhelmed

When asked about his friendships, Jeff remarked that he really didn't have any. Renee seemed to have many friends who were teachers and administrators, and he had several casual acquaintances at his job, at least he did until recently. They knew several parents of their children's classmates, but no one well. He could not call anyone a close friend. "What about Bill?" asked the therapist. Jeff thought of his fellow club members primarily as fellow car fanatics, not as friends. But he remembered Bill's concern, and he had received calls and cards from other club members. Maybe he had friends after all.

CONCEPTUALIZATION AND TREATMENT

When Jeff and Renee arrived at the hospital (a neighbor agreed to sit with the girls), they met the therapist in the emergency room. They soon moved to an examination room, where Jeff was given two depression questionnaires: the Beck Depression Inventory (BDI) (Beck et al., 1961) and the Hamilton Rating Scale for Depression (HRSD) (M. Hamilton, 1967). Jeff's scores of 31 and 29, respectively, confirmed his severe depression. With Renee waiting outside, the therapist also had Jeff discuss in greater detail the issues they had mentioned on the phone, particularly his suicidal thoughts. He had had vague ideas of suicide, but he hadn't really made a concrete plan, nor did he really intend to carry one out. He just wished he didn't have to go on anymore. They also discussed specific details of his symptoms. His depressed mood had been more or less continuous, and worsening, for the past several months, though he couldn't pinpoint exactly when he started feeling down. He never cried, but he usually felt hopeless and dejected. He had lost interest in his children and his beloved Chevys. His appetite, sleep, and sexual desire had all greatly decreased. He had never had a previous episode he would call depression, although from time to time he had felt down. Certainly he had never had any thoughts of suicide before. He could remember no evidence of depressive symptoms with any family member, though if there were any, he added, no one in his family would be likely to admit it. After this, a psychiatry resident performed a brief physical exam while a nurse took a brief medical history.

In consultation with the resident and the supervising psychiatry attending physician, it was agreed that Jeff met the *DSM-IV-TR* criteria for Major Depressive Disorder, Single Episode, Melancholic Type. Despite his severe depressive symptoms and his suicidal thoughts, it was agreed that he was probably not in any immediate danger of suicide. Jeff was started on paroxetine (Paxil), an antidepressant of the SSRI class at 10 milligrams per day, increasing to 20 the next week. Jeff was also urged to begin psychotherapy. He agreed and was scheduled for weekly sessions at the therapist's office. It was suggested that Jeff talk to his boss and arrange a brief leave of absence, two or three weeks, if possible. Before going home, Jeff signed a safety contract in which he promised to contact the therapist if he felt any suicidal urges, or, if that were not possible, to go immediately to the emergency room.

Jeff arrived at the first therapy session on time. He was neatly dressed, but he had prominent beard stubble, disheveled hair, and a look of complete exhaustion.

Initially therapy focused on interpersonal factors associated with the onset of his depression. From his notes, it struck the therapist that Jeff's depressive symptoms first began to appear shortly after his promotion to project manager. "Was there something," he asked Jeff, "about your job change that you found upsetting?"

"*Everything* was upsetting!" Jeff wailed. His responsibilities increased tremendously, but he felt no more authority. Now he had to answer for the performance of the entire project group, a group he felt little control over. Worse, he was expected to solve endless disagreements and squabbles within the group. He felt attacked from both sides. He described several instances of his boss's demanding explosions and his subordinates' near mutinies. Everyone, it seemed, was dissatisfied with him. And everyone was probably right. "Some people can manage," he reflected, "and some can't. I can't."

In the next session Jeff described similar interpersonal problems with his marriage, his family, and even his car club. He became vice president of the club, he explained, just to help out. But it turned out to be a repeat of work: once again he was saddled with the responsibility to settle personality conflicts without having any authority to do anything constructive. The therapist liked this example because the small size and limited involvement of the group made for a particularly simple and clear illustration. The first few sessions were devoted to gathering information about Jeff's depression, his interpersonal interactions, and his personal history.

At Jeff's third session, he reported feeling much less depressed and that his suicidal ideation had virtually ceased. These were good signs, for they indicated that Jeff was probably responding to his medication. His improvement also indicated that it was likely that he would continue treatment. At the end of this session, the therapist was optimistic. He felt he understood Jeff's situation moderately well, at least in a general sense, and Jeff seemed to be making good progress. It was time to clarify the issues that would be the focus of therapy and to make a therapy contract. The issues they would focus on would be his management role at work, his interpersonal interactions with his family, and his perceptions of what was and was not appropriate in various interpersonal situations.

At this point the therapist felt that the trust alliance had developed to the point where he was comfortable suggesting interpretations that could challenge some of Jeff's long-held beliefs. However, he was careful to avoid phrasing these interpretations in a way that diminished Jeff's sense of control in the therapeutic process. Instead, the therapist was careful to bolster Jeff's role within the therapeutic alliance while empowering him at work. He asked Jeff, "I get the sense that you care a great deal for your subordinates and want to help them. But it also sounds like you sometimes ask for their permission before you make decisions. Is that right?" From this gentle beginning, the therapist directed the discussion to the crux of the issue: Jeff's inappropriate—and ineffectual—adoption of a submissive role with his subordinates. He was gradually prodded to realize (and, eventually, suggest himself) that establishing himself as leader, issuing clear expectations, and holding employees responsible will work to everyone's benefit.

The therapist also discussed the opposite end of Jeff's work dilemma: his overly passive responses to his superiors. As he did with his subordinates (and apparently his father, older sister, and wife as well), Jeff habitually adopted a submissive interpersonal role. For example, one particularly humiliating experience occurred when his project group submitted an unusable design. Although the design flaw was clearly not his fault, he nevertheless took sole responsibility and apologized for the error. It is difficult to say whether this habitual submissive interaction pattern resulted from an immediate reaction to his superiors or from his habitual submissiveness, which prompted others to take control. In all likelihood both of these factors were at work. The end result was that Jeff trapped himself in a position where he accepted criticism of his work without question, yet he did not see any legitimate way to assert his own perspective. It is little wonder, then, that he felt helpless and worthless. Again, through carefully phrased interpretations, the therapist attempted to get Jeff to recognize his often self-defeating interpersonal style and to find ways to assert his proper authority. One particularly helpful technique was role playing. First the therapist would portray Jeff's role and model possible responses Jeff could make to his superiors. Jeff then played himself and practiced responses he felt might be particularly useful.

The remainder of the sessions during the middle stages of therapy were used to discuss interpersonal issues related to Jeff's marriage, family life, and interactions with his parents and sisters. Analyses of interpersonal exchanges and role playing were utilized throughout. Jeff was quite responsive to these techniques, and his depression continued to lift. He suggested that Renee accompany him for one or two sessions, and the therapist agreed. The possible benefits were that Renee would be more sensitive and aware of their marital dynamics, thus increasing the likelihood of maintaining gains after therapy. Renee joined Jeff for sessions 11 and 12. The therapist noted that Jeff was careful not to criticize Renee for her "bossy" behavior; rather he phrased the discussion in such a way that Renee was induced to discover for herself many of the communication patterns that characterized their marriage.

At session 14 the therapist brought up the issue of termination. Before doing so, though, Jeff again completed the BDI and HRSD, scoring 8 on each, which were well within the normal ranges. With this clear sign of improvement before him, Jeff was encouraged about his ability to remain well after therapy. The therapist mentioned that he would discuss Jeff's medication with the psychiatrist, given Jeff's clinical improvement. Following standard guidelines, antidepressant medication was continued for six months after he felt well to minimize the possibility of relapse.

At the final session Jeff and his therapist reviewed his progress over the last four months. Virtually all of his somatic complaints had ceased, except that his sleep was still somewhat disturbed. He no longer had suicidal thoughts. There were significant improvements in virtually all topics. He again spent evenings with the family and helped with family chores and duties, and his relationship with Renee was much improved. Although his job was still a source of moderate stress, he no longer found it overwhelming and is making plans to transfer to a position within the company with reduced management duties. And finally, as Bill corroborates, Jeff is back at his Tri-Chevy meetings. Although Jeff states that he has not regained the concentration and focus needed to resume the restoration of the Vette, he once again enjoys attending club events and just cruising around town with the Bel Air. Once again he finds fulfillment in the two loves of his life: his family and his cars.

PROGNOSIS

Jeff's prognosis is good. The development of a single episode following a stressful life event (his job change) is not unusual, and the course of his recovery is common for individuals who respond well to treatment. At termination he no longer met any criteria for depression. He has a stable and supportive nuclear family and no identifiable family history of mood disorders. It is possible that his successful therapy will provide some long-term protection, but this remains speculative.

Despite the factors in his favor, it is likely that Jeff will experience another depressive episode at some point in the future. *DSM-IV-TR* reports that the probability of developing a subsequent episode following a single episode is at least 60 percent, and the severity of his presenting symptoms argue that his chances of relapse might be higher still. Fortunately, his successful response to treatment means that effective measures are available should he experience a relapse.

A particular cause for concern is his avoidant characteristics, which are not likely to diminish over time. Interpersonally, it is possible, if not likely, that his avoidant personality will lead to persistent feelings of low self-esteem, which will translate to yet more self-defeating interpersonal encounters.

NEVER GOOD ENOUGH

PRESENTING COMPLAINT

Cindy couldn't believe the impact her father's death had on her. She wouldn't have believed she would grieve for him at all after suffering years of his physical abuse and emotional neglect. He was critical and domineering, but he really got violent during his alcoholic rages, which were frequent. But here she was, 5 months after he was put in the ground, and she just wasn't coping. She cried everyday, and her concentration was so bad that she could barely keep her mind on her job and her children. She was holding it together so everything looked good from the outside, but inside she felt drained and defeated.

There was little support available to her. Her husband, an inpatient and rather insensitive man, kept telling her to get over it. Of her three children, the eldest is in college and doesn't call often, while the younger two are preoccupied with their high school problems. She got some support from friends, but she had so little time for them. Finally she found relief when she joined a grief group at her church. During the first session, it came out that Cindy had never really been happy as long as she could remember. Her life was a process of trudging on by putting one foot before the other, with little thought as to her own needs or wants. With the urging of the group members, she scheduled an appointment with a psychologist recommended by her minister.

Case 8

PERSONAL HISTORY

For her initial interview Cindy arrived on time and was dressed neatly and conservatively. She is a woman in her early 40s who wore little makeup or jewelry. About 6 years ago, she began working outside the home as a secretary for a local landscaping service. She was quiet and reticent in her manner and had to be prompted to elaborate on many details.

Cindy grew up in a middle-class section of Denver. She is the eldest of four children, with a sister two years younger and twin brothers five years younger. Her father, who had died suddenly five months before, worked as an insurance adjuster. She described his negative, domineering personality and that he frequently flew into angry rages, but she avoided any mention of an alcohol problem. Cindy said that he often told her that she would never be happy or successful, and for the most part she believes him. Cindy saw her mother as someone who was caring and concerned for her children but ineffective in reducing her husband's rages. When Cindy was 12 her father left the family to move in with his secretary, whom he married after her parents were divorced a year later. Her mother, who had no skills and had never worked outside the home, suddenly had to earn an income and secured a retail job that required many hours away from home. Cindy took over much of the parenting duties for her younger siblings, making meals, doing laundry, and trying to enforce household rules. Always responsible and dutiful, Cindy had trouble controlling her sister, who got involved with drugs and sex at an early age. Her brothers were involved in sports and parties; they were not serious students like Cindy, but neither were they delinquents like Cindy's sister.

After graduating high school, Cindy worked at a film developing lab to earn money for college. However, within a year she had dated and married the store manager. She confessed in a later session that she had gotten pregnant and felt compelled to marry.

As it turned out, this was not a wise decision. It became clear over the next few years that her husband, Denny, had many of the negative characteristics of her father: he was a critical and insensitive alcoholic whose drinking gradually escalated over their marriage. He had struck her a few times early on, but his abuse was mostly verbal and emotional.

When her therapist asked about family psychiatric history, she guessed that Cindy's father was an alcoholic. "Yeah, how did you know?" Her family psychiatric history was positive for alcohol problems in her paternal grandfather as well as her father, and her sister had major severe problems as well. In addition, her sister had been treated for major depression and bipolar disorder and had made two suicide attempts in her early 20s. Cindy believes that her mother was depressed as well, though she never sought any formal mental health treatment.

Cindy's therapist also guessed that Cindy has felt pretty down for a long time, and that she probably had panic attacks at some point. Indeed, Cindy had panic-like anxiety attacks off and on since her teens; they were extremely distressing but never really debilitating. She had two or three since her father died. For most of this time she had also felt down, gloomy, and vaguely unfulfilled. "It's like there's no color; everything's gray, a blah feeling, you know?" She couldn't say exactly when she started feeling this way, but it was probably about the same time that she started having the anxiety attacks. She knows that she has had long periods of feeling down and empty for most of her adult life. She summed it up by saying that she has never felt validated as a person. Cindy was given the Beck Anxiety Inventory (BAI) and the Beck Depression Inventory (BDI), two 21-item self-report tests. She scored 15 on both, indicating mild to moderate anxiety and depression. Cindy had never really considered herself depressed, but she supposed that was the right term for it.

CONCEPTUALIZATION AND TREATMENT

Cindy's psychologist was able to guess the father's alcoholism and Cindy's prior anxiety attacks because they fit a pattern the psychologist has seen frequently in middle-aged women, particularly passive women with domineering spouses. Cindy's family fits the classic adult children of alcoholics (ACOA) pattern. ACOA children tend to be sensitive to a specific set of issues: having little control, difficulty developing trust, unfulfilled personal needs, exaggerated responsibility, denial of negative feelings. Almost always in ACOA families there is one child, usually a daughter and most often the eldest, who takes on the role of **The Hero,** who sees it as her duty to compensate for the failings of her parents (Cermak, 1986; Cermak and Brown, 1982). This child attempts to put up a good front for the family by getting good grades, excelling at sports or other activities, and caring for younger siblings, all the while getting little or no recognition in return. The Hero tries harder and harder to please the demanding parent, who never seems to be satisfied. In the process she instinctively learns to ignore her own wants and desires in order to serve her needy and demanding parents. A pattern evolves where the child is so used to being exploited that she takes it for granted and fails to even recognize her situation as exploitative. This process has been summarized as Don't Talk, Don't Trust, Don't Feel. Cindy's therapist puts it another way: "Life becomes a one-way street going *out*."

Besides the Hero, other children in the family typically take on the roles known as **The Rebel** (a behavior pattern aimed at getting attention through antisocial and/or unconventional acting out), **The Clown** (a child who attempts to diffuse family tension by acting immature or silly), and **The Lost Child** (an attempt to escape the family pain, mentally if not physically, by becoming withdrawn, apathetic, and depressed). Thus, knowing this pattern and hearing Cindy describe her family, it was no great leap to presume that at least one parent, probably her father, was an alcoholic.

Because Heroes automatically think of serving others instead of themselves, they often choose partners with complementary needs, that is, those who themselves expect to be served. It is no surprise that many of these partners are demeaning and controlling and often have substance use problems themselves. Much frustration and resentment build up over the years, but because Heroes are so self-sacrificing, they rarely express their anger directly but instead try to suppress it. It is not clear why this suppression occurs; perhaps Heroes don't allow themselves to get angry, or they may fear their partners' reactions, or they may not even be aware of their own anger. It's probably all of the above. In any case, this suppressed anger has no place to go, and a rush of anxiety often seems to be the result. It's almost as if the body is saying what the mind won't allow.

There is no *DSM-IV-TR* diagnosis for being a Hero. Officially, Cindy meets criteria for Dysthymia. Dysthymia is in essence a mild, long-lasting form of depression. The person must feel depressed mood for the majority of their time ("most of the day, more days than not") for a period of at least two years and without any period longer than two months without the symptoms. The depressive symptoms do not meet criteria for a major depressive episode or any other mood disorder. Cindy also has anxiety problems. Even though her current anxiety symptoms do not meet criteria for Panic Disorder, nevertheless her therapist will keep her anxiety issues in mind when she formulates a treatment plan. Finally, the therapist much keep in mind the issue that brought Cindy into treatment in the first place: her bereavement over her father. Cindy's long-standing depressive and anxious symptoms indicate problems that long predated her father's death; nevertheless, she still must remain aware that an important aspect of Cindy's issues involves her grieving.

In formulating a treatment plan, the therapist decided that, although Cindy has moderate depression and anxiety, since Cindy's issues were largely interpersonal, she preferred to hold off on medications and instead see if interpersonal psychotherapy (IPT) and cognitive-behavioral therapy (CBT) would be effective. She relayed this suggestion to Cindy's physician, who concurred. Often psychologists develop a good working relationship with primary care physicians. Of course, the physician has the ultimate responsibility for any decision involving medication.

At the end of the initial session, Cindy's therapist asked her to write a letter to her late father. In this letter she was to be open and honest, brutally honest, in telling him how he had hurt her and how angry she was at him. Cindy was to actually write a letter, not just make a list of notes or think of a letter in her head. When Cindy responded with a dubious look, her therapist explained that the letter had three purposes: First, it would give Cindy a way to vent the frustration she had been bottling up all these years. Second, by her actually writing the letter, the flow of negativity would be going from her to her father, rather than coming at her. Third, by acknowledging his faults and limitations, Cindy could eventually forgive him. Contrary to what many people believe, forgiveness is not for the sake of the forgiven, it is for the benefit of the forgiver, who can now let go of past anger. Cindy understood these points but still thought that writing a letter to a dead father was a little strange. She also felt very uncomfortable about the idea of expressing her anger, but she nevertheless agreed.

Initially she found it difficult to get started, but once she did begin, it was like a dam burst. She came to the next session with a six-page, single-space typed letter expressing her anger and outrage, and also relaying her sadness that they never developed a close relationship. To her surprise, Cindy found the exercise to be a cathartic release, and she felt more energetic than she had in years.

Another focus of therapy was to build up Cindy's self-esteem. To this end, she was instructed to begin reading David Burns' *Feeling Good*, a book the therapist often suggested for people with depressive issues and low self-worth. Another book the therapist recommends in these cases is Harold Kushner's *How Perfect Do I Have to Be?* CBT was employed to build up Cindy's self-esteem. Many CBT techniques were employed, a primary one among them being a discussion of cognitive distortions. People with depression almost always have thoughts and attitudes that are skewed in a negative direction. This phenomenon is called a Depressive Schema. People with depression tend to notice information in their environment that confirms their negative self-views. For example, they will ruminate over a boss's complaint but undervalue or even ignore that same boss's praise. One simple test the therapist has is to ask her patients how they respond to compliments. Most people with depressive schemas are uncomfortable accepting compliments. Another common distortion is to minimize the value of one's successes and to exaggerate the impact of one's failures. Yet another common distortion is to jump to negative conclusions. For instance, a single mistake may be taken as evidence of a major flaw ("I'm stupid" or "I'm incompetent"). By identifying these cognitive distortions, Cindy is more aware of how her own thoughts and attitudes may be negatively biased.

Another cognitive technique to build self-esteem is to use positive self-affirmations. Cindy was given a list of positive self-statements ("I'm smart"; "I can handle this"; "I'm generous") and instructed to rehearse this list at least twice daily and to use these affirmations whenever possible, even if she didn't quite believe it herself.

Finally, the therapist attempted to foster Cindy's assertiveness. One way was to ask Cindy what she did for fun, be it sports, hobbies, or whatever. Usually self-sacrificing people like Cindy have few or no personal interests; their attention is always focused on what they can do for others, not what they can do for themselves. By assigning her to engage in activities she finds pleasurable (and she had to be assigned), she gradually accepted the fact that she was worth special attention.

> **Therapist:** Tell me, what do you think would make you truly happy?
>
> **Cindy:** Well, Denny thought it would be great if we both started golfing more. He thinks that would make us both a lot happier.

Therapist:	Um, that sounds like Denny's idea. What about you?
Cindy:	Well, I don't know. I guess I try to be a good wife. I was always taught to be a good wife and have a great marriage. Those things were always really important. I guess that's what's expected of me.
Therapist:	Now it sounds like your parents talking. What about you, Kathy? What do *you* want out of life?
Cindy:	(pause) I have no idea.

Another aspect of increasing self-esteem is to refuse unreasonable requests from others. Over the next several sessions, Cindy had an almost endless string of episodes where her husband, her boss, her children, and even her friends were taking advantage of her. Cindy was urged to refuse these demands and instead demand fair treatment. She was warned that as she feels increasing assertiveness, her interpersonal systems (husband-wife, mother-daughter, boss-employee) will show a shift of power and be disrupted. In other words, as she gains power, these other people lose power, and they don't like it. These disruptions usually take the form of escalating complaints or criticisms from the other people. By anticipating these effects, Cindy was not only warned, but she could see these negative reactions as a positive sign—that she was indeed making progress. There is a stereotype in our culture that assertiveness training turns meek, subservient people into dictatorial tyrants. Although it may feel this way to the other people who are no longer easily able to exploit and control their partner, in actuality a passive person who receives assertiveness training tends to still be thoughtful and sensitive to others' needs, they just aren't so easily dominated as before.

Although Cindy initially came to therapy for grief work, it became clear from the initial session that the goals of her therapy were much broader and far-reaching: reducing her depressive and anxious symptoms by reducing her anger, increasing her self-esteem, and adjusting her interpersonal role in her relationships. These sorts of fundamental changes take time. At first Cindy saw her therapist every week. Then after many of the initial grief issues were resolved, therapy gradually became more spread out, to biweekly sessions, then to monthly sessions. After eight months, Cindy felt ready to discontinue therapy and return on an as-needed basis.

PROGNOSIS

Cindy's initial grief issues and associated depressive and anxious symptoms decreased rather rapidly. After three months, her scores on both the BAI and BDI were below 10, indicating minimal to mild symptoms. More gradually, she also experienced increased self-esteem, as evidenced by her asking for a raise at work and her picking out a car that her husband disapproved of both things that were unthinkable to her before therapy. All indicators for her continued progress look good.

Nevertheless, personality is an extremely stable entity that resists long-term change. It is quite possible that Cindy will gradually slip into her prior dependent-subservient interpersonal roles, especially if she is deeply threatened by the disruption in these systems. Still, she clearly has learned several valuable cognitive and behavioral skills that should help her maintain more equitable interpersonal relationships.

As a final note, therapists treating Heroes and others who are highly motivated to serve others must always be careful not to have the person become dependent on the therapist. An important part of teaching individuals to be more assertive and autonomous is to have them feel confident to handle their problems on their own. The therapist is no less a player in the person's interpersonal systems, and he or she must always remain cognizant of this relationship and the ultimate goals of therapy.

ROAD RAGE

The news is filled with cases of sudden, seemingly unprovoked violence. Bar shootings, hockey dads who assault coaches, and domestic violence are common occurrences. Certainly the most infamous case in recent memory was the trial of O.J. Simpson, a wealthy, charming retired football star who was accused of the sudden, brutal stabbing of his wife, Nicole Smith. Although he was acquitted at his criminal trial, the finding against him at a subsequent civil trial, as well as a history of numerous past and subsequent domestic violence complaints, has led many to question his personality and motives. Perhaps the most random, and therefore most frightening, form of spontaneous violence involves road rage. The majority of these people, almost all males, are usually regular men with jobs and families who one day snap in a blaze of anger and violence. There is much disquiet beneath their seemingly passive appearance; truly these men are ticking time bombs. What makes them tick?

PRESENTING COMPLAINT

As was his usual routine, Ron had just had two beers with his buddies after work and was driving home. Suddenly someone cut in front of his pickup. It wasn't really close enough to make him slam on his brakes, or even to brake at all, but he felt like the other driver was showing him up, and he wasn't going to take that. He rode up to within inches of the car's rear bumper, bright lights blazing and horn honking. Then the jerk in the car gave him the finger! That was it. He pulled ahead of the car and forced it off the road. He stormed back to the car, where the driver was yelling from his open window. Ron grabbed his arm and pulled him out the window, pushed him against the car a couple times hard enough to dent the door, and then began swinging. He was so mad that he hadn't noticed the woman in the car holding a phone, screaming for him to stop. Out of nowhere, a deputy sheriff car pulled up, lights flashing. This seemed to get his attention. Before he knew it, he was face down on the ground getting his hands cuffed behind his back. "But he cut me off!" was his only feeble comment before he was read his Miranda rights. He decided he should keep his mouth shut.

This wasn't the first time Ron was involved in a fight—far from it—but it was the first time he was ever arrested. Following the recommendation of his attorney, Ron pled no contest at his hearing in exchange for the prosecutor's recommendation of treatment in lieu of incarceration. The judge seemed to hesitate while she looked over some papers. Finally she said that since he had no prior convictions, she would sentence him to two years' probation. His probation contained the usual prohibitions against alcohol and drug use or any criminal arrest. He was also required to maintain steady employment. Furthermore, she ordered him to be evaluated at the Legal Diagnostic and Treatment Center, a group practice of forensic psychologists who treat mostly patients who are referred by the court, and he was required to fulfill the recommendations of this evaluation. And, she reminded him sternly, any parole violation would bring him back before her bench, and with the stroke of a pen she could have him serve the remainder of his sentence in the county jail.

PERSONAL HISTORY

Ron grew up in a working-class neighborhood of Toledo. There were 10 children in his family of third-generation Hungarian/ Slovak immigrants; Ron was the sixth. His parents were still married and still living in their modest 3-bedroom home; two younger brothers still lived with them.

Ron's father worked on the assembly line at Willys (now Jeep) for 30 years before his retirement. Now he worked part time as a bartender. Ron's mother stayed home to raise the children until the youngest was in middle school. Now she works part time in the high school office.

After high school, Ron went to work at Jeep, but he couldn't stand the boredom or the layoffs. After a few years, he landed a job with the department of streets for the City of Toledo and has worked there the last six years. This is a good job, good pay, good benefits, no layoffs so far, and the work sure beat the assembly line. He went for the promise of probation mostly because he knew he'd lose his job if he had to do any jail time.

When asked if there was any abuse or violence in his home during his childhood, Ron didn't know how to answer. The truth was that violence was a way of life. He remembers that when he was young, his father would often slap, push, hit, or beat his mother and his older brothers. His older sisters caught it once in a while, but that was less often. The family never knew when he might explode; almost anything could set him off. When he was drunk, though, there would almost always be some "action." Gradually his violence decreased over the years. It wasn't clear whether this was because he was mellowing out in his old age or whether he was getting older and weaker and couldn't intimidate his older sons any longer. Whatever the cause, by the time Ron was a teenager he got easy stuff like getting slapped, pushed down, or knocked against a wall, never the real beatings his two older brothers endured. What Ron said was, "Well, I don't know if I'd call it abuse. We got punished once in a while, but it wasn't too bad."

Ron was downright evasive when asked about his own history of violence. He admitted to a few fights in school and bars, "normal things." "What about at home?" he was asked. "Things were OK. I mean, no one ever called the cops on me." This wasn't exactly true. His criminal record included, besides a few traffic violations, an arrest for disorderly conduct six years ago, and another for domestic violence about four years ago. Notations stated that the case involving the DC was dismissed, and the charges were dropped for the DV. Ron was surprised the evaluator had this information, thinking that only convictions appeared in the record. He minimized these episodes, saying the bartender had mistaken him for someone else, which is why it was dropped later. He did admit that one time he had pushed his wife, and she had gotten scared and called the police, but that she had later realized she had overreacted.

CONCEPTUALIZATION AND TREATMENT

Ron's diagnosis was Intermittent Explosive Disorder. This diagnosis is among a category of impulsive-control disorders that include problems such as kleptomania (purposeless stealing), pyromania (fire starting), trichotillomania (hair pulling), and pathological gambling. Intermittent Explosive Disorder describes people who can't control their anger. To meet diagnostic criteria, the person must have a history of several episodes of violence against people or property that is seen as a gross overreaction to the situations that provoked them.

Intermittent Explosive Disorder describes Ron's behavior, but his attitudes and personality are also part of the picture. Underlying Ron's propensity toward violence are his antisocial and narcissistic personality traits. *DSM-IV-TR* defines a personality disorder as an enduring, long-term pattern of inner experiences (thoughts, emotions, beliefs, etc.) and behaviors (interpersonal cooperation, impulse control, etc.) that deviates from social expectations and cause problems with work, relationships, or mood. The person's responses tend to be inflexible and inappropriate. *DSM-IV-TR* defines ten personality disorders; among these are Antisocial Personality Disorder and Narcissistic Personality Disorder.

The essence of an antisocial personality is a pervasive disregard for the rights of others and a willingness to violate others' rights for one's own gain. This pattern can be expressed by unlawful behavior, deceitfulness, impulsivity, aggressiveness, recklessness, irresponsibility, and a lack of remorse. If the person demonstrates at least three of these characteristics, is over 18, and has had conduct problems as a child, then Antisocial Personality Disorder is diagnosed.

Narcissism is an inappropriate focus on one's self and a relative insensitivity of the value and needs of others. A person who demonstrates five or more of the following characteristics meets *DSM-IV-TR* criteria for a Narcissistic Personality Disorder: exaggerated sense of self-importance, preoccupation with unrealistic desires, belief in one's own specialness, need for admiration, a sense of entitlement, exploitation of others, a lack of empathy, envy of others, arrogance. In addition to these characteristics, many mental health professionals believe that narcissism is a dualistic condition: it is an outward shell of arrogance and cruelty that masks an inner weakness and fear. This is why, they speculate, narcissists react so violently when they feel slighted, disrespected, or their self-esteem is threatened in some way.

Does Ron meet these criteria? Although Ron tried to minimize his aggressive behaviors, it is clear from his record, his descriptions, and even his general manner that his behavior clearly warrants a diagnosis of Intermittent Explosive Disorder. With the only source of information being Ron himself, it is difficult to diagnose personality disorders. However, it is clear even at his evaluation that he has antisocial and narcissist traits, if not the full-blown personality disorders. This could be said for virtually everyone who is evaluated at LDTC.

Ron's evaluator recommended both group anger management classes and individual psychotherapy for Ron. Not wanting to violate his parole and risk losing his job, Ron reluctantly complied.

The anger management class was held once a week from 5:00 to 7:00 in the evening for 12 sessions. Occasionally someone will enroll in the class voluntarily, but most often they are court-referred. At the first week, 12 men and 2 women were in attendance.

Because of their antisocial traits, group members are constantly testing the limits of the group and its leaders. As a result, rules must be strict and rigorously enforced. Anyone who misses more than two weeks does not complete the program; anyone more than 15 minutes late is considered absent. There are no excused absences. "But what if I'm sick, or have an accident on my way here?" complained Ron. "That's what the two absences are for. So don't blow them now; you might need them later." Finally, there were weekly assigned readings, verified by brief quizzes at the beginning of class and/or homework assignments due at the beginning of class. There is a great deal of leeway given to these quiz results since the educational backgrounds of the members are so disparate.

After initial introductions, including brief accounts of the problems that got the members to the class in the first place, the first stage of treatment involved psychoeducation. The leaders discussed the nature, purpose, and appropriate uses of anger. Anger was not to be eliminated; it was to be managed into appropriate channels. If a person tried to ignore his or her anger, it just simmered, like a pot on the boil. Sooner or later they're bound to blow unless they can vent their steam in some way.

A second stage of treatment assessed the stressors that the members experienced every day. This helped to determine the provocations (called "triggers") in each member's life, which ones seemed worse than others, and when and how they provoked aggressive responses. The narcissistic nature of many group members meant that the group leaders had to carefully limit each member's narratives, or else the entire session would be consumed in recounting the stressors of the week. Sometimes it made sense to avoid triggers, especially the ones that really didn't matter. Sometimes you had to know they were coming so they weren't a surprise.

Third, work was done on developing a greater sense of empathy in the group members. By putting the group member in someone else's head, their natural assumptions of being disrespected or shown up were lessened. When it was Ron's turn, he was asked what the other driver thought. Did he really intend to cut him off? Maybe he was talking to his wife, or maybe he was playing with the radio, or maybe he dropped something, or who knows what. Was it really cutting him off at all? It's pretty self-centered, the leader reminded Ron, for him to assume he knows for sure what's going on in someone else's head or to assume, without doubt, that this other driver has nothing better to do than cut off strangers in pickups.

A fourth stage of treatment was to challenge the group members' externalizing of blame. For people with anger problems, it's always someone else's fault for what happens, never their own. These members think about their wives nagging; they don't think about forgetting to take out the garbage—again. They think about the boss being unfair; they forget about being late to work—again. When it got to be Ron's turn, the leader asked, "You told us before that the guy in the other car gave you the finger because he was a jerk. Ron, is it possible, just possible, that there was some asshole riding his bumper, flashing his brights and honking his horn!"

The final stage of treatment was to develop and practice appropriate responses to triggers. One useful approach demonstrated by the leaders was the Cognitive Interpersonal Therapy described by David Burns (Burns, 2002). Among other things, CIT involves (1) imagining the other person's point of view, (2) expressing one's own views openly, and (3) showing the other person respect, even if one completely disagrees. A useful technique to develop this skill was role playing. First, the leaders would model appropriate responses to threats posed by group members. Next, group members would respond to provocations instigated by the leaders. Finally, group members would practice appropriate responses to triggers with each other.

At first Ron was not a happy camper. At first he dismissed the value of the group as just "a bunch of psychobabble BS." He was certainly not alone in his derision of the classes. Most of the people taking the class talked, made jokes, and refused to cooperate. On the second week, most members were late, and only a few had done their homework. But once the group leaders handed out absences for these problems, the group members paid more attention and showed up on time with their assignments done—or at least attempted. Like everyone else, he felt relief when he described the various problems in his life at work and at home. As the class went on, he found that he was actually learning some things here and there. The one part of the group that had the most influence on him was watching a leader making use of CIT when Ron was trying to provoke him. He didn't lose his cool, didn't argue back. But he didn't seem intimidated, either. He said what he wanted to say without having to win.

> **Ron:** You know what I think? This is BS!
> **leader:** Oh yeah, Ron? How come?
> **Ron:** Well, it's just a waste of time. It's just so
> The city can make more money.
> **leader:** Interesting theory. So this is my plan to get
> rich, huh? So you saw my Lexus in the
> parking lot, huh? (laughter)
> **Ron:** Well, maybe not you. But the county.
> **leader:** Hmmm, maybe. But I doubt it. I mean, think
> of what it costs to pay for the deputy, the
> EMS team that took that guy you beat up to
> the hospital, the dispatcher who sent them,
> or the ER doc who patched him up. I
> wonder. Who do you think's out more, you
> or the county? But you may be right. What
> do you think?
> **Ron:** I don't know. Maybe not.

There were seven group members left by the twelfth week. This 50 percent dropout rate is fairly typical, although it would seem surprising, since for most members dropping out constitutes a parole violation, which could easily land them back in jail. But such is the impulsiveness, irresponsibility, and bad judgment endemic in this population.

Ron stayed with the program, missing only once, and graduated with a certificate of completion. He reported that he did learn a lot about himself and his relationships, especially CIT.

Ron followed up by attending the first three weekly individual sessions. The focus of these was to consolidate the gains made in the group sessions and to apply what he learned to various situations in his own life. Unfortunately, after his missed session, Ron came to a fourth session, then didn't return. After two more absences, his parole officer was contacted to inform her that he was not following through with his individual sessions as was technically in violation of parole. She thanked the therapist but didn't seem overly concerned. It is unknown what, if any, consequence Ron suffered for discontinuing individual therapy.

PROGNOSIS

The prognosis for Ron is poor. His discontinuation of individual therapy meant that his main, if not sole, motivation for seeking treatment was merely to comply with his conditions of probation. It is likely that he learned some valuable skills and techniques, and his relationship with his wife, children, and co-workers may have improved to some extent. But it is unlikely that his fundamental personality changed in any significant way, and over time he is likely return to his usual pattern of behavior.

Personality traits are very resistant to change unless there is some immediate consequence hanging over the person's head. It seems that once the fear of being jailed for parole violations (PV-ed in the lingo of the field), there seemed to be no internal motivation to make gains in his interpersonal functioning.

RIDING THE RELATIONSHIP ROLLERCOASTER

PRESENTING COMPLAINT

Debbie is a 34-year-old married homemaker. Her husband, Mark, is a 37-year-old corporate lawyer who specializes in international law. Debbie and Mark met each other 11 years ago, shortly after he was hired by her father's firm. They have been married for seven years and have no children. They divide their time among three residences: a lavishly decorated townhouse in Boston, a 14-room summer home in New Hampshire, and a large condominium in Zurich, where Mark stays during his frequent business trips to Europe.

The therapist made first contact with Debbie one afternoon in February when she called in a panic about a "marital crisis." She was clearly agitated and sounded as if she had been sobbing. After briefly introducing herself, she described her crisis. She and Mark had gotten into an argument just as he finished packing for a business trip. She accused him of abandoning her and began to insult and berate him. In the heat of the fight she threw several porcelain figurines at him, each one costing several hundred dollars. None had struck him or even come close. As she continued to fight with him, he slapped her with enough force to knock her off balance. She then started sobbing. When he saw that she was not injured, he began to leave. Debbie threatened to kill herself if he left her alone, but he walked out the door. After a little while Debbie called a friend. The friend was a former patient of the therapist and suggested that Debbie call him.

The therapist was extremely concerned over several aspects of the call. The first was the mention of suicide. He asked Debbie if she really wanted to die. She seemed a little surprised by the urgency in his voice. No, she said, she didn't really want to die. But she often got so angry with Mark that she said things like that. The therapist continued. Did she have a concrete plan? Had she made any previous attempts? When her answers were again negative, the therapist felt assured that she was in no immediate danger and did not require hospitalization.

He was also concerned about domestic violence. Debbie was taken aback by this phrase even more than the talk about suicide. No, neither she nor Mark ever really got hurt. Charges? Of course she had no desire to file charges. Once again convinced that there was no immediate danger, he arranged an initial consultation during lunch the next day.

Debbie arrived right on time. She showed none of the frantic emotion of yesterday; in fact, she was wary of the therapist, half suspecting that he was trying to take advantage of her somehow. But she decided to stay the hour. He also had his concerns. He began by asking her once again about her ideas of suicide and her feelings of depression. She repeated that suicide was a frequent threat. Yes, she takes too many pills sometimes, but she never went to the emergency room, and she really had no intention of dying. He then asked her about her mood. Had she been depressed? No, not really. Irritable? Maybe a little. Bored? Oh, yes. She said that for the last several years she has felt apathetic and lethargic. This was especially noticeable when Mark was away, but it persisted to some extent most of the time when he was home, too.

He then asked her whether she had spoken to Mark since their argument. She had called him on the way to the airport to apologize and to say how important he was to her. Mostly she didn't want him to worry. According to Debbie, this switch from anger to concern was common.

I have these lightning-fast changes in my feelings for Mark. It's like there's a little switch inside me that moves from NICE to MEAN. I remember one time when we took an elevator to a business party. I was feeling fond of him and proud of his success. But then, the moment he walked out of the elevator and into the hall, I suddenly hated him. I started saying that he only had his job because he married me, that he was living off my father's money. It's not true, you know; he's a brilliant lawyer. Anyway, I said that he was manipulating and controlling and arrogant. There we were in the hallway: I was yelling at him, and he was yelling back. We had to just turn around and leave the party. This happens all the time; I suddenly get mean and vindictive. I really worry that one day I'll just drive him away.

The therapist again asked Debbie about domestic violence. Mark struck her yesterday; had he hit her before? She replied that he had slapped her once before. It was a slap like yesterday's. She had also slapped him on occasion, but usually she throws things at him. She claims that she doesn't really want to hit him, and never really aims. "But I did bean him a few times by accident, of course," she giggled. Clearly, she wasn't worried about domestic violence, and she assured the therapist that the violence has never escalated beyond yesterday's level. The therapist then asked her about other aspects of their relationship.

Therapist: How is your sexual relationship with Mark?
Debbie: Do you mean how much or how good?
Therapist: Both.
Debbie: Well, it's pretty dismal. I guess we make love twice a month, on average. But remember, he's not home a lot.
Therapist: Do you enjoy it?
Debbie: He seems to, but I don't, really.
I don't think I was meant to enjoy it. I used to get excited by sex, but I haven't for a long time now. I feel like I'm sexually dead.
Therapist: Do you have any plans for a family?
Debbie: God, no. We used to talk about it, but we usually ended up fighting. I'd get so angry at him that I'd swear I'd never have his

children. You know, I've had two abortions.
I scheduled them for when he was away, and
I don't think he knows I didn't think he
deserved any. And then think of the money
they'll cost.

Therapist: Didn't you just say he was a good man,
"brilliant" I think was your word?

Debbie: You see, my mood can change pretty fast!

The therapist then asked if she ever hurt herself—like
cutting or burning herself. She seemed surprised that he would've
guessed, but yes, when she was in her teens and early twenties, she
did often cut herself along the arms and legs. But that stopped years
ago.

The therapist scheduled Debbie for two sessions a week. He
also called a colleague who specializes in Dialectical Behavior
Therapy (DBT) and referred Debbie to weekly group DBT
sessions.

PERSONAL HISTORY

Debbie is the oldest of four children. Debbie's parents are
from a poor manufacturing town in Connecticut. They were married
in their teens when her mother became pregnant with Debbie. For
the first few years of her life, Debbie lived in Cambridge,
Massachusetts, where her father went to engineering school. Soon
after graduating he founded a small company that designed and
manufactured medical equipment. This business has grown into a
large corporation with three plants in the United States and two in
Europe. Debbie's mother has never been employed outside the
home. Debbie describes her as a "professional hostess" who is very
involved in entertaining clients and socializing at company events.

Debbie describes her father as a strict, demanding tyrant
who gets his way through intimidation and reproach. He was very

proud of his rags-to-riches rise in business, and he expected his children to show similar successes. Debbie describes her mother as rarely showing Debbie any encouragement or compassion; she seemed consumed with trying to perform to her husband's stringent expectations and by her growing dependence on alcohol and barbiturates. None of the four children is close to either parent.

CONCEPTUALIZATION AND TREATMENT

Because interpersonal problems are so subjective, it often takes several sessions to recognize a personality disorder if you have information from only the person; problems in relationships and interpersonal interactions like work only come out gradually. But Debbie provided ample evidence to suggest a Borderline Personality Disorder right off the bat.

Borderline personality disorder is defined as a long-standing character disturbance marked by sudden and dramatic shifts in mood, unstable and intense relationships, and inconsistencies in the evaluations of oneself and others. *DSM-IV-TR* lists nine specfic criteria that define borderline personality disorder; a person must demonstrate at least five to warrant a diagnosis. Instances that fit each of these nine criteria can be found in Debbie's behavior. The nine criteria are:

1. unstable, intense interpersonal relationships
2. impulsiveness that is potentially self-damaging
3. unstable mood
4. inappropriate and/or uncontrolled anger
5. recurrent suicidal threats
6. persistent identity disturbance
7. feelings of emptiness and boredom
8. efforts to avoid abandonment
9. stress-related paranoid ideation

Borderline personality disorder is considered to be one of the most severe of all the personality disorders (Arntz, 1994;

Gunderson, 1996; Kroll, 1988; Linehan, 1993), and treating borderline patients is not a task for the faint of heart. They are extremely demanding in terms of the therapist's time and energy. Two issues predominate in treatment with borderlines. The first is establishing a therapeutic alliance. As Debbie's case demonstrates, this can be a difficult process. In fact, this case is a relatively uncomplicated example. Many borderlines are treated for years without establishing a positive alliance. Others make frequent inappropriate demands on therapist, such as late-night phone calls. One therapist received a phone call at home from a borderline client. His 10-year-old son answered, only to hear some stranger on the phone threaten to kill his father! Still other clients switch from therapist to therapist (or from hospital to hospital) in their efforts to avoid emotional intimacy.

The second issue that predominates in treatment involves transference and countertransference. Debbie's case provides a good example of the transference process. Because transferences are often negative and persistent, therapists must be especially careful in managing their own countertransference reactions.

Debbie is quite a provocative person, both in her physical attractiveness and in her hostile rages. Although her therapist is generally a very easygoing and calm man, she often brings out the worst in him. On several occasions her therapist felt like he "wanted to sock her." Although he does not condone the fact that Mark had struck her, after treating her for several months he understood Mark's frustration and even feels that Mark is to be commended for showing such restraint over the past 11 years.

In addition to the demands of building a therapeutic alliance and managing transference and countertransference reactions, therapists who treat borderlines must contend with three additional problems. First, change tends to be slow and gradual, and therapeutic plateaus are frequent. Second, borderlines are generally unable to project their thoughts into the future, and thus they often fail to grasp their own improvement and how it might have an impact on their lives. Finally, most borderline patients have limited ego strength and weak impulse control, and they have little reason to expect positive change.

Early in treatment, it was important to coordinate with the DBT group leader. Because of her trust issues and her fears of abandonment, as well as her sense of elitism, Debbie was very resistant to joining the group. She would often miss meetings, almost as a challenge to her therapist's authority. Finally her therapist set a limit where she was required to attend DBT group for him to continue seeing her. Though she complained and resented this requirement, she nevertheless began to attend DBT group regularly. Here she was taught cognitive techniques to raise her self-esteem and reduce her impulsiveness. She also benefited from discussions within the group, which helped her see issues more empathically while she was practicing her social skills.

In individual therapy, her therapist set up a structured, goal-oriented treatment program to cope with her immediate concerns. The first and primary goal of this program was to develop a trusting, therapeutic alliance. But as can be see above, establishing this trusting relationship with a borderline patient is easier said than done. However, once she developed a trusting alliance with her therapist, she was then able to focus on a goal-oriented program that directly addressed many problem areas in her life. Debbie's treatment program has five primary goals:
1. Improve impulse control
2. Increase self-esteem
3. Increase sexual contact with her husband
4. Reduce depressed mood
5. Diminish paranoid ideation

1. Improving impulse control. When Debbie began therapy, she had very little impulse control. This was expressed most dramatically in her sudden outbursts aimed at her husband, though it came out in other ways too, including shopping sprees and driving recklessly. One effective technique was to tap into Debbie's expressed interest in money. Once her therapist recognized this interest, he developed an economy metaphor. For each altercation with her husband, Debbie was to ask herself what it would cost her in terms of anger, bitterness, and Mark's potential rejection of her versus what she would gain from controlling her anger in terms of pleasure, self-esteem, and security. When she felt the need to castigate Mark, she was to stop and first calculate the costs and payoffs. Simply stopping to calculate this econometric helped Debbie avoid many of her impulsive behaviors.

2. Increasing self-esteem. Debbie's therapist found two ways to increase her self-esteem. The first involved focusing on Debbie's strengths, many of which had been glossed over. For example, Debbie works on many charity boards and organizations. She is very attractive and sophisticated, and she can be remarkably charming. As a result she is quite successful at fund-raising and dealing with corporate donors. However, she usually dismisses the value of her efforts by saying that it is "only" charity work. In therapy she was urged to recognize the value of her contributions.

A second approach to bolstering self-esteem was to diagnose specific conditions that Debbie had always interpreted as signs of general failure. Debbie's school history suggested the possibility of an undiagnosed learning disability. The therapist arranged to have Debbie tested by a specialist in learning disabilities, and sure enough, she met the criteria for mathematics disorder. By explaining her limitations as diseases, the therapist instructed her to no longer see herself as generally stupid but merely as someone who suffers from a rather common, specific learning disability, sort of like being nearsighted. And just as nearsighted people are prescribed corrective lenses, she was given some practical advice for how to live with her mathematical limitations, such as using a calculator.

3. Increasing sexual contact. As therapy progressed, Debbie occasionally described elements of her sex life that she found particularly pleasing. It turned out that most of these experiences occurred with her husband. These pleasant memories were pointed out to her to highlight the positive aspects of her relationship with him, which were often forgotten when she went into a rage and focused only on his negative qualities. The approach to increasing her sexual behavior took much the same form as the treatment to control her impulses. She was asked to think of how much a pleasurable sexual encounter was worth to her. What would she get out of it? What would Mark get? How would it contribute to their relationship as a whole?

Debbie was also encouraged to have open discussions with Mark about her problems with intimacy. In the beginning she was unable to tolerate more than a cursory exchange without feeling overly threatened, but at least Mark was beginning to understand that her somewhat hot-and-cold sexual behavior was not really meant as a personal rejection.

Progress in this dimension was somewhat erratic. Certainly the quantity of her sexual activity with her husband increased, but often she felt threatened by the increased intimacy and recoiled. This would be expressed by her making preparations for a sexual encounter (making a special dinner, buying new lingerie) but then suddenly deciding to sleep in a different room, leaving her husband confused and frustrated. But even this was an improvement. In the past she would drive Mark away with a stream of hostile remarks when she felt threatened by intimacy. More and more, she signaled her refusal to have sex by relatively benign behaviors. Only when she began to make real progress did she really come to accept the intimacy that comes with sex and show a significant improvement in the quality of her sex life.

4. Reducing depressed mood. Aside from Debbie's rather alarming mention of suicide during her initial telephone call, she showed few overt symptoms of depression. As therapy progressed, however, a consistent pattern of dysphoria began to reveal itself. Although Debbie remained fairly active socially, she regarded many of these activities as dull and monotonous. It became clear that most of her everyday activities were initiated by friends, relatives, or other external demands, such as business dinners and deadlines for charity drives. Much of her boredom and apathy stemmed from her identity

97

disturbance: until she developed a coherent sense of self, the events in her life continued to lack meaning.

Debbie was referred to a psychiatrist for a medication evaluation, and he prescribed the antidepressant bupropion (Wellbutrin), which increased her general activity level and her interest in her outside activities. It also improved her willingness to complete some of the treatment recommendations suggested by her therapist. Not unimportantly, unlike most antidepressants, Wellbutrin is very unlikely to decrease her sexual drive.

5. Diminishing paranoid ideation. Sometimes Debbie's wariness of intimacy and her desperate need not to be abandoned combined to produce behaviors that had a paranoid quality. One indication of her deep mistrust was her extreme jealousy, expressed by her frequent accusations to Mark of his "screwing around," to use one of her least vulgar terms. While it was true that Mark's travel schedule and long hours provided him with ample opportunity for extramarital affairs, in actuality he had never given Debbie good cause to doubt his fidelity. Nevertheless, she frequently confronted him with jealous accusations. At a recent dinner dance, Debbie saw a coworker whom she suspected was one of Mark's lovers. Mark made no comment concerning this woman; in fact, he hadn't even known she was at the dance. Suddenly Debbie began sobbing and making quiet but audible comments that she "knew all about that bitch." Mark quickly led Debbie out. A loud argument began in the hallway and lasted through the ride home. In therapy Debbie admitted that Mark had given her no reason to suspect this woman, but still Debbie could not control herself.

Another sign of Debbie's paranoid ideation was her manner of holding grudges. Once Debbie called her therapist to reschedule an appointment she had to miss. He was ending a session with another patient at the time and asked her to hold for a few minutes. She hung up 30 seconds later. Being familiar with her inflated sense of entitlement, he was not particularly surprised by this. But he was surprised when she brought up this phone call four weeks later as evidence that he habitually takes advantage of her.

The therapist's method for having Debbie gain control over her paranoid ideation had two steps. First, Debbie was asked to analyze as objectively as possible the evidence that supports her suspicions. Second, she was reminded that her accusations were not "free"; they carried certain costs, such as embarrassing and aggravating the accused as well as starting a hostile interaction. She was told to be responsible for her accusations. Together these suggestions had the effect of making Debbie think before pointing her finger, which greatly reduced the number of impulsive rages.

When Debbie began therapy, she was always prompt and attentive. Gradually, however, she began arriving late—first by a few minutes, but then by as much as half an hour. After three months she began skipping an appointment now and again, and then after four and a half months she discontinued therapy for a period of three weeks.

Up to this time Debbie and the therapist had made great gains toward establishing a therapeutic alliance; Debbie's comments became more open, revealing, and personal. At the same time, her level of hostility toward the therapist gradually increased. She never failed to question the latest bill he sent her, even though nothing had changed since the first one. But the most interesting expression of her hostility toward him was her grooming habits. It began when Debbie brushed her hair during a session. She brushed her hair again at the next session, but this time she pulled the hair out of the brush and let it fall on the couch. She quickly began to perform more and more of these grooming habits, and with each one the residue left behind wound up on the therapist's couch: used tissues, cotton balls, and even clipped toenails. The therapist became more and more annoyed, but he suppressed his anger and tried as best he could to remain cool and professional. Finally he decided to point out this behavior and discuss its underlying meaning.

Having been a fashion model, Debbie was careful to manage her appearance. She would be particularly careful with a male authority figure, whom she would naturally associate with her hypercritical father. By putting on makeup in front of the therapist,

Debbie symbolically conveyed that she was willing to have him see the real her without her first needing to cover her faults. But by leaving her litter behind her, she was also asking him to clean up her garbage. Thus, she saw him as both savior and servant. As they developed a closer alliance, however, she felt threatened by the increasing intimacy and tried to drive him away, in this case with her rude, inconsiderate behavior. She was transferring her ambivalent feelings about her father, and to a lesser extent her husband, onto the therapist. She needed him to accept the real her, yet she feared that he might abandon her once he saw her faults. Her behavior was a test to see what he would put up with and how much he really cared.

When the therapist discussed this transference reaction with Debbie, she reacted with a blank look. She was unaware of performing her grooming behaviors, let alone their underlying meaning. Though she had no immediate reaction to his interpretation, she seemed to think about it as she left. She arrived on time for the next session and has attended regularly ever since. At the next session she was very interested in the concept of transference and the way it revealed her underlying motives. Whether this experience will lead to a significant and lasting behavior change remains to be seen.

PROGNOSIS

Debbie has been in therapy for about eight months, and her therapist is optimistic about her prognosis. She has many innate strengths, including a high IQ and an engaging manner. She was successful in establishing a therapeutic alliance, and she has begun to be more tolerant of intimacy with her husband. Her impulse control problems have diminished markedly, and they will most likely continue to recede. Most noticeably, her self-esteem has improved. She was never as severe as some of the members of the DBT group, who have had multiple suicide attempts and still practice self-harm, so compared to this group, at least, her outlook is positive.

Still, personality disorders are notoriously persistent, and doubtless many problems will continue. It will take a number of years before she matures emotionally and is able to accept her hostile and libidinal urges. Until then, she will remain dependent on a man, both financially and emotionally. In addition, she will be limited by her learning disability, though she has learned to make allowances for it.

NEVER TOO YOUNG TO QUIT

PRESENTING COMPLAINT

It had been an insanely wild summer. Grace had gotten drunk and high virtually every day, if not every single day. She and Conrad (Rad) had a cool bunch of friends who shared a daily ritual. They'd get up around noon, usually with a hangover, and get together in the afternoon. They would get high and make plans for the night. At 10:00 or 11:00 p.m. she would sneak out to meet them, and they would spend the night getting high. On what? Almost every night there was drinking, and most nights they smoked marijuana. Otherwise is was what someone had handy; ecstasy and acid were common, cocaine sometimes, and occasionally prescription drugs like Ritalin, Adderall, or Oxycontin. Maybe they would go to some clubs, or maybe they would just hang out. Rad would (hopefully) drive her home around 4:00 a.m., when she would crash, limp and wasted. But by noon the next day she was ready for more. It was fun and exciting.

But it could be dangerous, too. Rad didn't always manage to take her home. About a month ago he had left her at a club in San Francisco's seedy SOMA district (he had either gotten mad at her or just forgotten her, neither could remember which), and she stumbled around the warehouses and bars for three hours wearing only a ripped T-shirt. Finally a security guard, fearing she might have been raped, called SFPD, who took her to a local hospital. When the police were satisfied that she had not been assaulted, they called Grace's mother to pick her up. Her mother, who thought Grace had been safely tucked in bed, was flabbergasted. Grace earnestly protested that it was the first time she had ever done anything like that and promised that it would never happen again.

Her protests weren't necessary; her mother was too frightened and confused to think of punishment.

Grace decided to cut down on how much she drank and to cut out the drugs altogether, and for a few days she did. But soon her daily intake of alcohol was back up to her usual amounts, if not more. After a few more days she started smoking pot again, then using ecstasy and acid, and within two weeks her drug use was up to its old level.

Then one night she had a strange, almost spiritual revelation. It was a typical party-frenzy night just like any other, and she was intoxicated as usual, but it kept bothering her that she didn't quit drugs when she wanted to. While she and Rad were driving to yet another club, she asked him why she couldn't stop, why she gave up on her plan so quickly, why she kept getting high every night. Rad, who was a veteran of many Alcoholics Anonymous and Narcotics Anonymous meetings, knew what the answer was. Like him, she was an alcoholic and a drug addict, and she was obviously in denial herself. His answer, "Because you can't control it. Duh!" stated what was obvious to everyone who knew her, except, of course, Grace's mother and Grace herself. The simple truth of Conrad's statement turned on a light in her head, and for the first time it struck her that she might have a problem. If she really wanted to quit drugs, Conrad added, she'd have to quit everything. And she couldn't do it herself; she would need an intensive program, and probably detox too, and then some recovery group like AA or NA. "Well, Rad, since you know so much about it, how come you don't quit?" Conrad thought for a moment, "I guess I just don't want to, or maybe I can't."

Grace took what he said to heart, and he seemed affected too. She entered a rehabilitation program at a local hospital; Conrad entered a similar program across town. Both were typical programs: a few days of detoxification as an inpatient, then as an outpatient for an intensive multi-stage program. For Grace, Stage 1 involved psychoeducation and group meetings five times a week, Stage 2 stepped down to three times a week, and Stage 3 met once a week and focused on skills training and relapse prevention.

One component of treatment that began on the first day was attendance at AA meetings. Grace was surprised that there was no indoctrination, no twelve-steps lecture, no pressure to confess. The only awkward part was at the end of the meeting, when everyone formed a circle, held hands, and recited the Lord's prayer. The speaker at Grace's first AA meeting was a young woman, about 25 years old, who introduced herself by saying, "My name is Pat, and I'm an alcoholic." "Hi, Pat!" was the traditional, friendly refrain. Pat described a life of alcohol and drug use that gradually escalated into a series of uncontrollable binges. She had made three attempts to quit at rehab programs. At the last program she met a terrific man; they were married six months later. On their wedding night they celebrated by ordering a bottle of champagne with dinner. Then they ordered another, and then split a bottle of whiskey before passing out. Within a week they were both drinking everyday, and soon they started using drugs again; she tended to hold back, but her husband engaged in frequent cocaine binges. Then one night about three months ago he had a massive heart attack and died. This week would have been their first anniversary.

At the meeting the next day, three speakers got up and described lives ruined by drugs and alcohol. (Grace learned that these speakers are called "leads.") Other meetings introduced the AA Twelve Steps and the Twelve Traditions, and after these Grace picked up some AA literature and read through it in her room. She felt a sense of connection with the group almost immediately.

Grace's mother assumed that once Grace graduated from her outpatient program, her treatment was over. "Oh, no," Grace replied, "sobriety is a lifelong struggle." Then Conrad, newly graduated himself, came by and drove her to a meeting, leaving a startled mother behind. When Grace got home, her mother forbade her to attend any more meetings. She said she didn't want Grace to be around Conrad, whom she considered to be the cause of Grace's drug use in the first place, who was such a bad influence. But really she refused to see young Grace as an alcoholic, and she had a vague fear that she would lose Grace to a fanatical, cultlike group. She also forbade Grace to see Conrad. Grace and Conrad were undeterred, however, and they developed a system of code names and neutral pickup locations so they could continue attending meetings every day. When he drove her home, he made sure to park at least two blocks from Grace's house. After attending a couple of meetings at one of the groups, Grace approached the meeting organizer, introduced herself, and said that she would like to get up and talk. The next week she told her story. Although most of the meeting veterans thought they had seen it all before (and most had), still many in the audience felt a lump in their throats when a small Chinese girl walked up to the front of the room and lowered the microphone to her level. In her high, wavering, but determined voice, she announced, "My name is Grace, and I'm an alcoholic." She was 13 years old.

PERSONAL HISTORY

Grace is the youngest of three children. Grace's parents are both second-generation Chinese. Her father, a successful importer who now owns a chain of three small leather goods shops, abandoned the family when Grace was 4 years old, and she has little recollection of him. Ever since the separation, Grace's mother has supported the family through her job as a secretary for an importing firm in Chinatown, where she met her ex-husband. Despite help from her family and friends, being a single mother has been difficult, as evidenced by their moves within San Francisco: first from the elegant townhouse in Pacific Heights to a six-room apartment in the Marina, and then to a modest bungalow in the Sunset District. For the past six months Grace's mother has been dating a buyer for a local department store who does business with her company. Grace describes her relationship with her mother as "kinda distant."

Grace's sister is extremely intelligent but has always been a rebellious child. She has frequent fights with their mother over a variety of topics, ranging from dating and drug use to clothing and hairstyles. Her oppositional disposition is not solely instigated by her reactions to authority; she has just as many arguments with her siblings.

Grace's brother is also rebellious, but his quest for autonomy takes the form of aggressive behavior and drug abuse. He has not been as discreet or judicious as Grace, though, and his drug use has resulted in more serious brushes with the authorities. He has been suspended from school on three occasions, once for fighting and twice for having drug paraphernalia. He has also been arrested twice, once for vandalism and once for drug possession. His sentence for the latter was mandatory enrollment in an inpatient detox/rehab program and one year of weekly AA meetings. He was sober less than 24 hours after his release from detox, and he attended few AA meetings, usually while intoxicated.

Grace met most of her friends, including Conrad, through her brother. This put her in company with peers three to five years her senior. She mostly saw them only at night and on weekends. Grace developed a pattern of drug use she termed her "double life." She never used drugs while she was in school or with her mother, and to most authority figures she was the picture of innocence. According to Grace, if she just showed up on time where she was supposed to be, she was never suspected of anything. Her active masquerading even overcame incriminating evidence. Once her teacher noticed drug paraphernalia (a bong) in her purse and confronted Grace and even informed her mother. But Grace explained that her brother must have put it there as a joke, and she was readily believed. Grace's mother had other warning signs, such as finding some marijuana and condoms in her room, but again Grace shifted the blame onto her brother.

Grace's innocent public image contrasted with her nighttime persona. Grace had her first alcohol when she was 10 years old. When her mother had gone out and left the children home alone, they raided her liquor cabinet and got drunk. Soon after this she met her brother's friends, and they started going out together. At first she mostly had beer, malt liquor, and cheap wine, but gradually she became less discriminating, drinking whatever was available. She began to spend more and more time getting drunk with her brother's friends. Then boys in the group introduced her to pot. Starting from there, Grace quickly increased the frequency and variety of her drug use. By the time she joined AA, Grace used pot, ecstasy, and LSD

107

regularly, and she dabbled with other substances, including speed, hashish, cocaine, and prescription drugs.

Grace was on acid when she had her first visit to the hospital emergency room at age 11. She doesn't remember the event. Apparently while she was tripping she cut her wrists with a carving knife at a party. Her friends were terrified and called an ambulance. The wounds themselves were superficial, but the suicidal implications were very serious. She saw a psychologist once a week. Her therapy had little impact on her substance abuse; she was still seeing this therapist when she entered her intensive outpatient program.

Grace also experimented with sex. On most nights she had sex with Conrad, but they were by no means monogamous. She often had sex with other friends, and sometimes with strangers. Sex was usually unprotected. When she thought about it, she got very scared: scared of getting pregnant and scared of catching herpes, or AIDS, or God knows what else. She didn't like being scared, so she got high, which led to more sex, which caused more fear, and the cycle continued.

Denial also obscured her mother's view of Grace's behavior. Despite Grace's hospital emergency, finding Grace with drug and sex paraphernalia, and watching Grace come home drunk and high, her mother never suspected any serious drug use. Between the financial and family strains of single parenting, her new romance, and her difficult first two children, there was little opportunity for close supervision. Grace's mother expressed her utter surprise at their first family session: "I still can't get over that we're here because of Grace. She was the one I *didn't* have to worry about."

CONCEPTUALIZATION AND TREATMENT

Grace demonstrated a clear case of substance dependence. For over three years she had gotten drunk and high every weekend and many weeknights. Of all the substances she abused, she pointed to alcohol as causing most of the problems in her life, and alcohol dependence became the focus of treatment. The *DSM-IV-TR* criteria for alcohol dependence are (1) tolerance, a need for more alcohol to get the same level of intoxication, (2) withdrawal, symptoms experienced after discontinuing use or the need to take more of the substance to counteract withdrawal feelings, (3) consumption in larger amounts and/or more often than intended, (4) unsuccessful attempts to cut down, (5) a great deal of time spent obtaining, using, and/or recovering from alcohol, (6) social or recreational activities given up, and (7) continued alcohol use despite knowing it may cause physical or psychological problems. It is possible that Grace met all seven criteria. She failed to quit her alcohol use, or even to cut down on her alcohol consumption; she usually drank more than she intended, often passing out in strange places; she spent every afternoon and night getting drunk; she limited her social sphere to her drug-using friends; and she continued to drink and use drugs even after two hospital visits which she herself had attributed to complications from drug use. Over the course of her drug use, she gradually increased the amount of alcohol and drugs she consumed, until by the time of her treatment she was using amounts that would have killed her only a year before. But these fine points of diagnosis were lost on Grace. She was an alcoholic, plain and simple.

Grace quickly learned the process of recovery according to AA, which is summarized in The Twelve Steps. These first appeared in *Alcoholics Anonymous* (usually referred to as *The Big Book*) in 1939. They are:

1. We admitted we are powerless over alcohol—that our lives had become unmanageable.

2. Came to believe that a Power greater than ourselves could restore us to sanity.

3. Made a decision to turn our will and our lives over to the care of God *as we understood Him*.

4. Made a searching and fearless moral inventory of ourselves.

5. Admitted to God, to ourselves, and to another human being the exact nature of our wrongs.

6. Were entirely ready to have God remove all these defects of character.

7. Humbly asked Him to remove our shortcomings.

8. Made a list of all persons we had harmed, and became willing to make amends to them all.

9. Made direct amends to such people wherever possible, except when to do so would injure them or others.

10. Continued to take personal inventory and when we were wrong promptly admitted it.

11. Sought through prayer and meditation to improve our conscious contact with God *as we understood Him*, praying only for knowledge of His will for us and the power to carry that out.

12. Having had a spiritual awakening as a result of these steps, we tried to carry this message to alcoholics, and to practice these principles in all our affairs.

These twelve steps, in turn, are based on the Twelve Traditions, first printed in 1945. A short form of the Twelve Traditions, used commonly today, is as follows:

1. Our common welfare should come first; personal recovery depends on AA unity.

2. For our group purpose there is but one ultimate authority—a loving God as He may express Himself in our group conscience.

3. The only requirement for AA membership is a desire to stop drinking.

4. Each group should be autonomous except in matters affecting other groups or AA as a whole.

5. Each group has but one primary purpose—to carry its message to the alcoholic who still suffers.

6. An AA group ought never endorse, finance, or lend the AA name to any related facility or outside enterprise, lest problems of money, property, and prestige divert us from our primary purpose.

7. Every AA group ought to be fully self-supporting, declining outside contributions.

8. Alcoholics Anonymous should remain forever nonprofessional, but our service centers may employ special workers.

9. AA, as such, ought never be organized; but we may create service boards or committees directly responsible to those they serve.

10. Alcoholics Anonymous has no opinion on outside issues; hence the AA name ought never be drawn into public controversy.

11. Our public relations policy is based on attraction rather than promotion; we need always maintain personal anonymity at the level of press, radio, films.

12. Anonymity is the spiritual foundation of all our Traditions, ever reminding us to place principles before personalities.

AA is often described as a self-help group, but Grace disagreed with this label. "It is *group*-help," she explained, "You don't stay sober by helping yourself, you stay sober by helping other alcoholics. Besides, you depend on a Higher Power to get better. You can't do it yourself."

By the time Grace gave her lead, she had attended 25 AA meetings. But this was just the beginning. Grace would go on to attend at least one meeting every week, often two, for over nine months, totaling more than 80 meetings, and she has continued to attend meetings at least once a week until the present day. The content of the meetings varied somewhat, depending on what kind of meeting it was. Open meetings typically featured one, two, or three leads who described their experiences. Other meetings involved discussions of the Twelve Steps, while some provided opportunities to work in pairs or small groups and practice the steps, a process called "Twelve Stepping."

In addition to simply attending, Grace became involved in the actual running of the AA meetings. She started by offering to help set up, making sure the seats were arranged and the literature was stacked and available. Next she volunteered to make the coffee, an indispensable ingredient at any AA meeting. Next she became the anniversary person, who kept notes of the members' sobriety durations for small award ceremonies held during the meetings. Eventually she took on the task of arranging leads and other speakers, both within the group and from other groups. After three years she was asked to give inspirational speeches to other groups. With money provided by the AA General Service Office, she toured the country delivering talks describing her own experiences, particularly to younger audiences. She also encouraged existing groups to be especially accepting to young alcoholics in their groups.

Contact with fellow AA members wasn't limited to the meetings. Grace has called her sponsor at his home during particularly stressful occasions, especially in the early phases of her recovery. Although she felt vulnerable during periods of loneliness and depression, for Grace the hardest time to remain sober was when she felt good and wanted to have fun. This feeling of joy brought up many drinking cues, since many of her most joyful experiences involved alcohol and drugs. She also knows many fellow alcoholics who relapsed just when they were improving. She thinks that the satisfaction, joy, and relief from gaining control over one's life makes people want to celebrate, and for many people, as Pat described in her lead, celebrating means drinking and using drugs, which starts the addiction cycle all over again.

In addition to AA, something that had been helpful for Grace was a local clubhouse. In Grace's case it was an apartment in a local building, but she knows of other clubhouses that are rented storefronts, separate houses, and other places. The clubhouse offers young people who want to abstain from drugs a place to go and hang out. Although not officially affiliated with any AA group, most of the people who go there are in AA or NA.

Grace's steady involvement in AA did not mean that she did not experience crises in her recovery. The first occurred right away, when she first learned about the Twelve Steps. At first Grace found the spiritual and religious overtones of AA difficult to accept. Her family had never been regular churchgoers, and she had many personal doubts about the existence of a supreme being. This is a fundamental hurdle to overcome, since AA is based largely on submitting oneself to the will of God. Grace was able to reconcile this issue by seeing AA's meaning of God as metaphorical, referring to some generalized external spiritual power. Gradually she came to accept this view and then to rely on it. "Although the AA meetings and sponsors help," she said, "sometimes there's only the Higher Power between you and that drink."

Another problem was that Grace's mother at first refused to let her go to AA meetings, basing most of her objections on Grace's renewed relationship with Conrad. After about three weeks, though, it became clear that Grace was seeing Conrad anyway, and she could detect a noticeable improvement in Grace's attitude. Convinced that AA was helping, her mother joined Al-Anon (an AA-type group for people who are affected by someone else's drinking) and met Grace for occasional family sessions with a counselor. Following the recommendations of the family counselor, the mother maintained a dry house. Now she and her boyfriend drank only while out, and just this change cut their drinking significantly. Over the years Grace's relationship with her mother and (later) her stepfather steadily improved, though she was never as close with them as with her friends at AA.

Conrad precipitated a crisis period when he began drinking and using drugs again after three months of being sober. Grace didn't want to stop seeing him, but it was too hard to be around him and his friends when they drank and used drugs, so she broke off their relationship. One of the first rules of AA is to change "people, places, and things" that have become associated with substance use and now threaten sobriety. This can be extremely difficult.

A final source of difficulty lay in the demographics of AA members. Grace described herself as having "three strikes against me" at the meetings: she was young, female, and Asian. *The Big Book* made it clear from its first printing in 1939 that AA should pose no racial, class, sex, religious, or any other barriers to potential members, and, at least in theory, AA welcomes everyone equally. This policy was remarkably progressive for its time. But the reality is that AA was developed by two white middle-class men in a time of relative social conservatism, and this beginning, combined with its puritanical tone, often led to members in some groups developing socially conservative attitudes. Although no one said anything openly derogatory to Grace, she often got the sense that older members just did not take her seriously. After all, how much life experience can a 13-year-old girl have? This same feeling of not fitting in has led to the formation of several organizations that cater to particular populations; those relevant to Grace include Women for Sobriety, National Asian Pacific Families Against Substance Abuse, and Narcotics Anonymous. Grace has spoken at meetings held by each of these groups, but she does so with mixed feelings. On the one hand, she wants to reach as many people as possible. On the other hand, though, she dislikes the idea of splintering AA into separate special interest groups. In the spirit of the Twelve Traditions, she thinks it is best to try to educate and broaden the views of all alcoholics instead of setting up demographic divisions.

Grace is now a junior at the University of Southern California, where she majors in psychology and works as a research assistant in the Institute for Health Promotion and Disease Prevention Research. She remains involved in two groups and goes to an average of one meeting per week. She does not contemplate any end to these activities; as she told her mother, for the alcoholic, sobriety is a lifelong task.

PROGNOSIS

In general, the prognosis for AA treatment is dismal. Research studies estimate that only between 5 and 13 percent of treated alcoholics will maintain a lasting AA membership; and usually when they drop out, they relapse. Another indicator of a poor prognosis is Grace's "three-strike" status, which would tend to make it more difficult for her to identify with AA groups. Although AA has become more accepting of younger members, female members, minority members, and drug-addicted members, still they can be fairly conservative in their approach. Knowing nothing else about the case, the prognosis would be poor indeed.

But more is known about this case: specifically, Grace's personal characteristics. Researchers report that the single most important factor in the success of AA groups is the personality of the individual. Here is where Grace shines, for she possesses virtually every desired trait. For one thing, she voluntarily sought treatment long before she reached anything approaching "rock bottom." Although her drug use had resulted in some significant interpersonal problems and some frightening episodes, it never disrupted her schoolwork, nor had it ever caused any serious legal or health problems. Grace is flexible in her attitudes and tolerant of others. She is outgoing and willing to disclose her faults. She is intelligent, energetic, and organized. She is free from other psychopathology, such as depression or character disorders. Typically, alcoholics share five negative personality characteristics: immaturity, impulsivity, irresponsibility, a sense of entitlement, and an externalization of blame. She is goal-oriented and views helping others as her primary task. She takes responsibility for her actions and avoids blaming others. Finally, she is motivated by a personal spiritual revelation, which keeps her going in trying circumstances. In short, Grace has the personal characteristics tailor-made for successful AA experiences. As of this writing she has been sober for seven years, and she remains very active in the program. Grace is likely to become a star within AA, but of course she will remain anonymous.

SHOOTING UP

Certainly one of the most well known opioid addicts was the eccentric billionaire Howard Hughes. At the time of his death, his Obsessive-Compulsive Disorder was widely known, as was his abuse of prescription medications. What was not so well known, however, was his morphine addiction. Physicians looking at x-rays taken during his autopsy were surprised to see dozens of broken needles still in his arms, legs, and groin. He first received morphine while recovering from a plane crash in 1946, and he remained an addict for the remaining 30 years of his life. For someone like Hughes, who had no regular job and no financial concerns, an opioid addiction had surprisingly little impact on his day-to-day functioning. But as we shall see in this case, for someone who needs to work for a living, such an addiction will jeopardize his work, his family, and even his life.

PRESENTING COMPLAINT

John is a 30-year-old mechanic who lives in a middle-class neighborhood in Philadelphia. He has been married for nine years and has two daughters, ages 8 and 5. For the past seven years John has worked as a heating-ventilation-air conditioning (HVAC) mechanic at a large city hospital.

John demonstrated superior job performance when he first began working at the hospital. He was known for doing a thorough and conscientious job, and he had a knack for motivating others. After only two years on the job, the manager of the maintenance department decided to promote John to supervisor at the first available opening. Over the last few years, however, John's performance has gradually deteriorated. Starting in his third year at the hospital, John began arriving late for work and leaving early, first only once or twice a month, but then once or twice a week. Verbal reminders went unheeded. Eventually John's supervisor filed a written reprimand. At this point John asked to work the night shift, and his supervisor agreed, glad to have John be someone else's problem. For a while John's punctuality improved somewhat, but gradually it deteriorated until he was rarely on time. Then John began to miss work altogether. At first he missed work once or twice a month, but eventually it reached the point where he showed up for work less than half the time Being the night shift, this behavior wasn't noticed right off until his coworkers got tired of always covering for him. Surprisingly, the actual quality of his work, when he did it, had not suffered much over the years.

John's supervisor tried to be understanding. He asked John if he had any special health problems or personal issues going on, but John was vague and evasive. Finally his supervisor became exasperated and instituted the formal three-step dismissal proceedings required by the union. The first step, a verbal warning, had occurred months ago. Now John was called into his supervisor's office and given a written warning, which outlined exactly what the hospital expected in terms of his attendance and productivity. John seemed rattled at this, and for the next two or three days, he did as expected. But soon his tardiness and call offs began again. Finally he was suspended. Knowing that the next step would be termination, John consulted Desmond, the coordinator of his union's employee assistance program (EAP). Desmond looked over his work record and asked, "What the hell's going on, John? What are you on?" Now, with nowhere left to hide, John described his addiction to heroin. Desmond had seen the signs many times before with other employees, and he had already contacted a residential treatment center. "It's an intensive addiction treatment program. You're in the hospital for a week, then it's follow-up from home, starting all day, every day. John, you're going to see them today." John was taken aback, stammered that he had his family, his house. "John," interrupted Desmond, "I'm calling the program at noon. If you're not there, don't bother coming back here. Understand?" Desmond then called John's supervisor. Without any explanation, he said that John would be absent for one month and that his performance should be reevaluated one month after his return. John duly went to the program for an evaluation and was admitted the following Monday.

PERSONAL HISTORY

John grew up in a predominantly African American working-class neighborhood in Philadelphia. His father was a moderately successful electrician who maintained steady work through one or another of the many contractors he knew. He was a longtime member of the electricians' union and had become increasingly active in union politics over the years. He died suddenly of a massive heart attack a little more than two years ago. John's mother has never worked outside the home; she is supported by Social Security and a small monthly annuity from her husband's union death benefit. John is the oldest of three brothers. He attended vocational school, where he did well. His youngest brother graduated from a local community college and now manages a retail clothing store in downtown Philadelphia. His middle brother has been in and out of jail since he was 15 and is now in a federal penitentiary serving a sentence for drug trafficking.

John's father was a large man who was prone to alcoholic binges. Occasionally while drunk he would beat his wife or one of his sons, but usually he was good-natured and jovial. He rarely disciplined the boys for staying out late or drinking; in fact he seemed more amused than angry when one of his sons came home drunk. John's mother was a quiet, passive woman who abstained from alcohol and other drugs. She was often upset about her husband's drinking binges but never confronted him directly. She was alarmed when she began to notice signs of drug use in her children, but again she did little to intervene.

119

John began to experiment with alcohol and marijuana when he was 11 years old. These drugs were readily available at his middle school, and many of his friends were daily users. John gradually increased his use of alcohol and marijuana throughout middle school. By the time he entered high school, John drank to intoxication on most weekend nights and sometimes during the week, and he smoked marijuana an average of three or four days a week. Toward the end of middle school John and his friends began to experiment with other drugs, including amphetamines, cocaine, barbiturates, hallucinogens, and heroin. John continued to use all these substances off and on throughout high school; he most frequently abused alcohol, heroin, and, to a lesser extent, marijuana.

John remembers first trying heroin when he was 15. A friend brought a small amount to a party, and he and several other friends took turns snorting the white powder. The calm feeling of euphoria was similar to the effect of marijuana but more potent; he found that heroin combined with alcohol produced an especially intense high. Over the next few years John bought and snorted ever-increasing amounts of heroin until he found it difficult to find enough money to support his habit. He then began selling heroin and other drugs to fellow students.

During this period John spent a great deal of time buying, selling, and taking heroin and other illegal drugs. On many days it was difficult to get out of bed, and sometimes he didn't go to school at all. Even when he did go, he usually spent an hour or more in the school yard talking to dealers, pushers, addicts, and friends who had dropped out. His truancy rate increased year by year, and his schoolwork suffered accordingly. Fortunately for John, he had always been an above-average student, and although his grades were dropping, he still managed to graduate on time and enter a vocational school.

The vocational school was across town, and John spent much of each day either commuting to school or at the school itself, which cut down on the time available to socialize with his drug-using friends. Also, his brother first went to jail at about this time, and this got him to back off his drug use. He still used on the weekends and occasionally during the week, but he felt he had control over his drug use. After he completed his training, he got a job working for a heating contractor. About a year later John married Sharon, a woman he had met on the bus while he commuted to the vocational school; their first daughter, Natalie, was born about a year after that. Eighteen months later, John was hired in his current job, and soon afterward they bought a modest house in a quiet, residential neighborhood near the hospital. They had a second daughter, Cicely. During this period of time, John's heroin use remained steady at about three or four times per week, but now it was less for the high than to ward off the withdrawal effects. He still used alcohol and marijuana now and then, but for the most part he stopped taking other drugs. John felt he had his life together.

Soon after John began at the hospital, his coworkers invited him to join them for a drink on the way home. At first he would stop for a drink once or twice a week, but this soon became a daily routine. John began to drink more and more and to linger at the bar later and later, eventually until long after his coworkers had gone home. John then began to frequent different bars. He made new friends who used marijuana, cocaine, and heroin in addition to alcohol. In this supportive atmosphere, his heroin use increased dramatically, to three, four, or more times a day. And for the first time in his life, John began to take heroin by injection.

John began by injecting heroin subcutaneously (under the skin), but soon progressed to injecting it directly into a vein. With each step, from snorting to subcutaneous injection to intravenous injection, came a dramatic increase in the intensity of the euphoric experience. Sometimes he would combine the heroin with amphetamines or cocaine into "speedballs" in an effort to heighten the euphoria and blunt the inevitable crash of the withdrawal, but he didn't really like the edge these stimulants put on the high.

An ever-increasing part of John's time was consumed by his drug use: obtaining drugs; recovering from highs, crashes, and binges; and actually taking the drugs. He couldn't come to work until he had an injection, and he had to have another during lunch break. If he didn't have any heroin, he had to find some. He had to shoot up again in the afternoon, and often left work early for this reason. John spent most evenings buying, selling, and taking drugs. This basic pattern continued after he changed to the night shift, except that now he had most of the day to sleep and engage in his drug activities. He began going to shooting galleries, run-down apartments or abandoned buildings where ten or more heroin users would share their highs. Needle sharing was common, as was casual, unprotected sex. In his more sober moments John realized the dangers of this risky behavior, but all caution was lost during the high. On most mornings John came home to crash before going out in the afternoon. His night schedule worked out well for him; he came home after Sharon and the girls were gone, and he left again before the girls got home from school. Often he didn't come home at all.

Not surprisingly, John's drug use led to severe financial problems. Because he was on an hourly wage, his absentee rate resulted in his bringing home less and less money. As his habit became more and more expensive, more of what he made went to his drug habit. Soon the family's modest savings were gone. Then he began selling items in the house: the wedding silver, the family stereo, the VCR. When Sharon asked about these items, he said they had been stolen. Still bills went unpaid, and sometimes there wasn't enough money to buy groceries. Sharon demanded to know where all the money was going, but she never received an answer. Three years ago she had gotten a job as a secretary at the local school, but even so they couldn't keep up with their bills. They frequently borrowed money from both sets of parents, often saying that one of the girls was sick. After about a year Sharon's parents refused to lend them any more money. John then turned to his mother and brother, and he continued to get money from his mother after she was widowed.

Eventually John began to sell drugs, mostly heroin but also some cocaine, marijuana, and amphetamine. Usually he acted as a lookout for a dealer, but sometimes he was involved in the actual buy. He bought a 9-mm automatic on the street, which he kept loaded and took almost everywhere. He was very careless with the gun; sometimes he left it out within reach of the children. Fortunately he was rarely home when his children were awake.

Although John's poor work performance directly prompted his referral, his family had also suffered greatly over the past several years. It began gradually. John would stop off at the bar more often and come home later and later. He would miss dates he and Sharon made with friends, and he forgot promises he made to his children. Sharon became increasingly frustrated and depressed by his withdrawal from her and their children, and she wanted to know where he went all the time and where he spent all his money. She suspected that he had a problem with alcohol and perhaps other drugs. She was fairly sure that he was having sex with other women and figured that he was spending some of his money supporting one or more mistresses. She yelled, begged, threatened, pleaded, and cajoled him to tell her, but her efforts failed. John even managed to turn her accusations around and put the blame on her, accusing her of being needy, suspicious, and unattractive. Often their fights ended with violence. Her relationship with her own family had become strained because of their constant borrowing, and now she felt alone and helpless. On several occasions she threatened to leave him, and twice she and the girls even packed up some luggage, but she could never go through with it. Eventually she resigned herself to her existence and tried to take care of their daughters as best she could.

CONCEPTUALIZATION AND TREATMENT

DSM-IV-TR lists several types of disorders associated with drug use: intoxication, withdrawal, abuse, and dependence. The first two involve acute responses to a psychoactive substance; the latter two involve established patterns of drug use. Although John suffered from repeated instances of heroin, alcohol, and cannabis intoxication and heroin and alcohol withdrawal, it was his long-term drug use that brought him in for therapy, and this became the focus of treatment.

Psychoactive substance dependence involves ongoing problems in controlling the use of a drug. The person exhibits cognitive, behavioral, and physiological symptoms related to drug use, and the person persists in using the drug despite the negative consequences associated with its use. *DSM-IV-TR* outlines seven criteria for diagnosing psychoactive substance dependence; a person must meet at least three to warrant a diagnosis:

1. marked tolerance
2. characteristic withdrawal symptoms
3. substance taken more than the person intended
4. persistent desire or unsuccessful attempts to control use
5. much time spent acquiring or recovering from the substance
6. social, occupational, and recreational activities are abandoned
7. continued use despite knowledge that use is harmful

Substance dependence is categorized as having physiological dependence if either criterion 1 or 2 is met.

We see from John's history that he fulfills several of the criteria for alcohol dependence, cannabis dependence, and opioid dependence, and his treatment is aimed at these problems in combination. However, in the last few years John's heroin use has predominated and has led to extremely risky behavior. For these reasons, his therapy team decided to focus their initial work on John's heroin use.

John was admitted to a 7-day residential treatment program located in a newly remodeled 25-bed ward in the hospital where he works. Just last month John replaced a thermostat in the group room here, and he wondered if he'd ever go here. Well, here he was. The program is voluntary. Nevertheless, the program has some inviolate rules. Any instance of physical aggression or violence, sexual activity, or drug use (checked through periodic urine screens) results in immediate dismissal from the program. In addition, the program has a very structured daily routine, and the residents are expected to participate fully.

The staff consists of a treatment director, three full-time treatment counselors, clinical nurses, and two night staff people.

The staff is firm but friendly; they try to instill a sense of structure combined with an atmosphere of fairness and understanding. Staff and residents are on a first-name basis. Since about 80 percent of the staff members are in extended recovery themselves, they can well empathize with the residents. Still, every member of the staff is highly trained and holds a Chemical Dependence Counselor Certificate (CDCC-III).

The program begins with detoxification, which takes place during the week of inpatient treatment. Yet even during the typically agonizing detox process, the residents are expected to participate in the highly structured treatment routine. The treatment approach is based on the Minnesota Model, so called because it was developed at St. Mary's Rehabilitation Center in Minnesota. This approach involves three aspects: changing drug behavior, tapping emotions, and restructuring living patterns. The goal of the program is not merely to end current drug use; it is also to make drug use less likely in the future. To achieve this goal, the addict must undergo a fundamental life change. Thus, the aim of the program is to restructure the habits, routines, cognitions, attitudes, and social environments of the addicts—in short, to change the entire lives of these addicts. It's a tall order.

Many short-term changes can be accomplished on the ward, but lasting change after graduation requires an alteration in the person's social environment. For this reason the involvement of family members and intimate friends becomes an integral part of the treatment process, and the staff tries very hard to get the addict to sign a release that will allow these other people to participate. Like most addicts, John was hesitant to get his family involved in his treatment. He felt embarrassed, ashamed, and guilty over how he had been mistreating his wife and daughters. His drug use had been the source of hostility between him and his family, and the program was likely to generate even more conflict as his wife learned the full extent of his drug use. This prediction proved to be accurate. Nevertheless, the staff strongly encouraged him to get his family involved, and he finally relented. Sharon was similarly hesitant to get involved, but the staff also convinced her that her participation would be beneficial, even crucial. Most residents of the treatment center eventually agree to involve their family, but despite the best efforts of the staff, some never do. Likewise, most family members do whatever they can to aid the recovery process, though in some cases family members want nothing to do with the addict and flatly refuse.

For this week of residential treatment, John's daily routine was:

7:30 wake up, get dressed, make bed
8:15 breakfast (attendance required of all residents, eating or not)
9:15 lecture
10:15 group therapy
12:00 lunch
1:15 lecture
2:15 group therapy
4:00 supervised walk around the neighborhood
5:15 dinner
6:30 lecture
8:00 Twelve Step meeting, often with outside speakers
9:00 homework assignments, free time (the only time TV is on)
11:00 bedtime

During the week John missed some of the scheduled activities because he suffered symptoms of alcohol and heroin withdrawal: a craving for more heroin and alcohol, trembling, sweating, diarrhea, racing heart, fever, insomnia, running nose, watery eyes, weakness. In fact, aside from the drug craving, John's withdrawal symptoms felt like an incredibly severe case of the flu. His withdrawal symptoms gradually subsided within the week. Although John was expected to follow the daily routine despite his symptoms, the staff made allowances here and there. John's roommate, a crack addict, had a much sharper withdrawal course. Within a few days he became depressed, irritated, and agitated; his cravings for crack were obvious and desperate. However, the staff made few allowances for him and forced him to conform to the daily schedule right from the start. The staff had learned that instilling a sense of structure is paramount in treating cocaine dependency, and it must begin immediately, despite any withdrawal reactions.

John was assigned to a therapy group with seven other addicts, and each of them seemed to be as desperate as he was. Bill and José had just lost their jobs; Hector, Steve, and Curtis were suspended or on probation. Maggie's husband threatened to file for divorce and seek custody of their son. Joe was referred by his psychologist. Bill and Curtis were longtime alcoholics. José was a polyabuser who had a long history of taking heroin, amphetamines, cocaine, crack, alcohol, barbiturates, and marijuana, apparently with little particular preference. The rest had also abused a number of different drugs, but their predominant dependence was crack. During the first two weeks of treatment, the group members gradually revealed their secret stories of cruelty, violence, and prostitution. Most incredible of all, John realized that his story was just as horrific as theirs, and maybe even worse. Throughout his life John had always thought that he was in control of his drug use, even during the last few months. But now he could no longer deny his addiction. For him, this self-revelation was the most agonizing part of his treatment. But this was just a taste of things to come.

After the first week, the program shifted to intensive outpatient treatment. The group continued to meet for 5 days a week, 9:15 am to 4:00 pm and continued the schedule begun in residential treatment. The addicts were urged to attend a Twelve Step meeting every day, but they had to attend at least 3 times a week to stay in the program. José was not there. During the week, Steve and Bill tested positive for cocaine and alcohol, respectively, and they were asked to leave.

The third week of the program is known as family week, when family members are asked to join the addicts in the treatment process. On Monday, Tuesday, and Wednesday, the morning activities are replaced by education classes that describe the disease model of addictions, using lectures, guest speakers, and films. Instead of the usual afternoon activities, the addicts and their families engage in "fishbowl exercises." The fishbowl exercises are run like group sessions, but with two important differences. First, the families of the addicts are now in the group, along with the usual group members. To keep things down to a manageable size, usually no more than two families participate in any single exercise session. Second, the addict is placed in the center of the group, where he or she becomes the focus of the entire session (and is in the "fishbowl"). On Monday the addict must remain quiet while family members take turns describing how the addict had affected their lives. On Tuesday the family must remain quiet while the addict explains the drug use from his or her perspective.

On Monday morning John was surprised to see his mother and brother accompany Sharon; she had not mentioned this at an earlier visit. Although everyone said they were happy to see him, their interactions were awkward and strained.

The session began with John in the fishbowl. Everyone was very hesitant at first, and their group counselor, Rick, had to do a lot of prodding. Sharon began by saying how much she had missed John these last few years. She saw him very little, but even then he seemed to be a different person. John's mother and brother agreed that he had changed. Sharon continued that the girls missed their daddy. Natalie in particular wanted to know what she had done to make him not love them anymore. John felt a lump in his throat and tears well in his eyes, but Sharon was just starting. She said that John was a monster to live with; he always criticized, blamed, and belittled her. They never had any conversation that wasn't a fight, and they shared very few activities. When they had sex (she looked up at his mother but then continued), it was more of a punishment than anything else. He was so impossible to be with that Sharon was glad when he started working the night shift.

John was surprised at Sharon's hostility, and he was also surprised at how much she knew about his drug use. She saw the needle marks in his arms and knew that he used heroin or cocaine. She knew that he had sold their silver, stereo, and VCR for drug money. She knew that he carried a gun and probably sold drugs. She knew that he slept with other women and wondered if he supported any mistresses. Sharon then demanded to know what she didn't

128

know already. "Who are those men I see you with in the morning?" "How much junk do you use?" "How many women are you screwing?" Although John was supposed to be quiet, he was allowed to answer direct questions. He didn't. The therapist marked down these questions to ask tomorrow. Finally, the session reached a crescendo.

> **Rick:** Sharon, tell John what makes you most angry about his behavior.
>
> **Sharon:** Angry? Angry? You know what this bastard did?
>
> **Rick:** Talk to *John*, Sharon.
>
> **Sharon:** You . . . I can't look at him. (She puts her face in her hands and sobs openly. She continues, looking at the floor.) You know what the worst of it is? Do you? It's that you made me feel like this was all my fault. And the girls, too. You know, Cicely never really knew you; she thinks you were always like this. But Natalie's old enough. She remembers how you used to be, and she thinks it's all her fault that you treat her like that. I just can't believe how selfish you've been to treat us like this. I don't know why I care about you. I've asked myself a thousand times. I feel so weak and stupid. I hate my life; I hate *you* for making me so miserable.

Sharon sat with her face in her hands and sobbed for another few minutes. John noticed that his mother and brothers were also looking down and holding back tears. He couldn't hold back his own.

Rick helped John up, and Maggie replaced him in the fishbowl. John didn't notice much about what was said. He was too upset by the last half hour. He also dreaded tomorrow; he knew that would be even worse.

And he was right. This time Maggie was the first one in the fishbowl. John watched her husband sullenly look on as she described the history of her addiction to crack. The low point came when she described having sex with drug dealers in her own home while her husband was at work. This was more than her husband could bear; he simply got up and left the room.

On this glum note, John entered the fishbowl. The group members were there to provide encouragement, but also to correct any glossed-over accounts; there was no need for either. John simply and plainly narrated his long history of drug use, from middle school experimentation to his suspension from work. Sharon cried when he described his frequent casual sex, and a look of horror came over her when he described the shooting galleries. But the biggest shock of all came toward the end of his story.

    Rick: John, what's the worst thing you did because of your heroin addiction?

    John: I guess it was shooting at that cop and the other guy at a bust. (At this, Sharon's jaw dropped.)

    Rick: Did you hit them?

    John: You just shoot, you know. You don't stick around to see what happens. They didn't come after us, though.

    Rick: Is that what you feel worst about?

    John: I should, but no, not really. I never really thought about it much; I guess I never thought of much of anything except for myself. But sitting here thinking about it, I guess I feel worst about what I did to Sharon and Natalie, and Cicely, too. I never thought they'd blame themselves. Hell, I never thought about them at all. I remember, after the drug bust, I came home and put the gun on the table. The girls were home from school, you know. And I just thought, "I hope one of them picks up the gun; they'll never trace *those* prints." Thank God they had enough sense not to get near it. But I mean, that's how I thought. I didn't think that they might get hurt or anything. God, how can anybody get like that? How did *I* get like that?

On Wednesday afternoon, the residents and their families made concrete plans for activities they could share that would replace the time spent in drug activities. Movies, trips to an amusement park, and other events were planned with the children, including a summer vacation. Two nights a month were set aside for a date with Sharon. John even agreed to attend church. And he consented to be tested for HIV. John kept going to his Alcoholics Anonymous (AA) and Narcotics Anonymous (NA) meetings. For her part, Sharon pledged to support John in these changes, and she enrolled in Al-Anon and Nar-Anon.

The treatment program continued for one more week. At that point, every resident who had completed the program was given a medallion as a tangible sign of his or her effort and work. Each graduate was enrolled in a two-year aftercare "growth group," a weekly two-hour meeting that provides support to recovering addicts and their families.

PROGNOSIS

It is difficult to provide a definite prognosis for John. His treatment program keeps no records on relapse rates, so it is impossible to estimate John's chances of remaining sober based on the performance of other graduates. The program does know that about 65 percent of its graduates remain in the growth group for the full two years. This does not necessarily mean that all 65 percent remain abstinent (in fact, that is doubtful). But it is a rough guess as to the number who at least maintained the sense of responsibility required to keep up with the growth group.

Because most treatment programs are voluntary and dropout rates are so high, true relapse rates are difficult to determine. Most estimates place the one-year relapse rate at about one-half to two-thirds.

John returned to work on a new shift and no longer associates with his drug friends. Also, John has entered his thirties, a time when most heroin users begin to reduce their drug use. Even with these positive changes and his continued weekly meetings, it is more likely than not that John will quit the program and use heroin again within a year. A likely fate for him is that his experience in treatment will allow him to recognize his addiction sooner and be more willing to seek help. In his case, like so many cases of addiction, success may best be measured in relative terms rather than black-or-white success or failure.

IS VIAGRA ENOUGH?

PRESENTING COMPLAINT

Jim is a 52-year-old single account manager living in Santa Monica, California, a suburb of Los Angeles. He has had many relationships over the years, but he has never been married and has no children. In addition to his regular job, he frequently auditions for various roles in television shows and commercials, and so far he has landed bit parts in two movies. On the whole, though, he assesses his acting as a hobby.

For the past few years, Jim has experienced sexual problems when dating. He went to his primary care physician, who gave him a prescription for sildenafil (Viagra), and this helped sometimes, but not always. At work he doesn't share these kinds of problems, but once in a while this topic has come up in conversations with other actors while waiting for auditions. Last week a fellow actor he had known for some time suggested that he see a therapist for his problems and provided him with a recommendation.

At his first session Jim appeared to be somewhat hesitant and awkward. He looked off in the distance when he described himself, and he occasionally stammered and giggled nervously. After several minutes, though, he became a little more relaxed and described the precise nature of his sexual problems.

For the past three or four years, Jim suffered from what he termed off-and-on impotence problems. Sometimes he had trouble maintaining an erection during intercourse, and he estimated that he successfully achieved orgasm "only about half the time, maybe less." Sometimes he achieved penetration but then lost the erection soon after. Often he lost tumescence upon attempting penetration, thus being unable to complete intercourse. Occasionally he failed to achieve an erection altogether. These difficulties were most problematic during intercourse; oral or manual stimulation brought him to climax more regularly, and masturbation almost always resulted in orgasm. Things were better with Viagra, but still he had problems with erections, especially during intercourse.

Jim stated that his sexual problem was compounded by what he perceives to be an overemphasis in the African American culture on masculinity and sexual prowess. He said that the women he dates, both black and white, expect him to be a terrific lover. He felt that his behavior was inadequate in comparison to this relatively strict standard, both in his own eyes as well as in the eyes of his partners. His partners usually felt frustrated and hurt when he lost his erection. Most blamed themselves and wondered whether they were not exciting enough or skilled enough. One partner felt so upset that she locked herself in his bathroom and cried for several hours. Most of his partners have not expressed their frustrations directly, although two or three have said that their evening with him was disappointing. This problem had been a considerable source of anxiety for him over the past few years.

Jim was also concerned about the effects of these problems on his sexual relationships. Because of the embarrassment and anxiety he felt as a result of his disorder, he often felt ambivalent about initiating sexual encounters for fear that he would not be able to perform. Jim was convinced that his disorder was the primary cause of his inability to form lasting romantic relationships, and this realization made him anxious and depressed.

PERSONAL HISTORY

Jim grew up in a working-class household in Los Angeles. He has two older brothers and a younger sister. His parents, neither of whom had finished high school, held a number of different unskilled jobs while Jim was growing up. Jim could not think of anything unusual about his childhood. He summed it up by saying that his parents were "good people; they worked hard and always had food on the table."

Jim described himself as a reliable, responsible worker who has done well for himself. He has had several long-term relationships. He has lived with several different women, but for one reason or another things didn't work out. He states that he would like to be married, but he just never found the right person.

Most therapies for sexual problems begin with a sexual history. Jim's sexual history also showed significant instability. He became sexually active at age 14 and described his sex life in high school as "successful." He has had many female sexual partners since then; he estimates the total number at around ten or twelve a year when he was younger, but now maybe two or three a year. For the most part he met his sexual partners through mutual friends, at work, or while auditioning for acting parts. He and his partners typically engaged in sex very early in the relationship, often in the course of their initial encounter, usually at his urging. Some of these became one-night stands, but usually he attempted to establish relationships with his sexual partners. In most cases, though, the relationship ended abruptly after only a few weeks. He guessed that the number of times he ended the relationship is about equal to the number of times his partner did. As he grew older, he became more selective in his partners, and he allowed the relationship to develop before initiating sex. For the past several years, the tables have turned, and his partners often pressure him for sex. He usually dates divorced women. He has dated a few married women, but "that's not my style." At the current time he sees two or three women casually but is not in a steady relationship.

When asked if he practices safe sex, he took on a guilty, defensive tone. "No, not really. You know, it's tough enough for me without those things (condoms) making me numb." Despite the relatively heightened awareness of HIV infection within the entertainment industry, rarely did a partner mention safe sex; no partner had ever refused an encounter on these grounds.

CONCEPTUALIZATION AND TREATMENT

According to *DSM-IV-TR*, the somewhat redundantly termed Male Erectile Disorder (usually abbreviated ED) is a sexual dysfunction characterized by a persistent or recurrent failure to attain or maintain erection until the satisfactory completion of the sexual activity, and that this failure results in distress and/or interpersonal problems. This diagnosis is not warranted if the dysfunction occurs only during the presence of some other disorder, such as a major depressive episode. In addition, *DSM-IV-TR* asks clinicians to specify (1) whether the disorder has been lifelong or was acquired after a period of normal sexual functioning, (2) whether the disorder is generalized to all situations or is specific in nature, and (3) whether the disorder is the result of psychological causes or a combination of psychological and physiological causes. (Erectile dysfunctions with a clear physiological cause are usually diagnosed as due to a general medical condition and/or substance-induced sexual dysfunction.)

Jim's primary complaint was that he lost his erection, and in some cases his sexual interest, during intercourse. This had been a cause of much anxiety and frustration for him as well as his sexual partners. He has no identifiable illness or pattern of drug use that would explain his problems. Thus, his complaints match the criteria for male erectile disorder very well. Clearly his dysfunction was acquired, since he had been having sex for many years, and his symptoms began only a few years ago. His problem appeared to be situational, that is, specific to intercourse; Jim was able to complete the sexual act approximately half the time and was consistently able to masturbate to ejaculation. Furthermore, treatment with Viagra was only partially effective. Given these factors, it was very likely that his disorder is psychogenic, that is, due to psychological factors.

Jim appeared to be a good candidate for therapy. He was open in his descriptions of his actions and his feelings. Although he described his problem almost completely in behavioral terms, he was nevertheless responsive to the suggestions and interpretations as to how his personality and thoughts may contribute to his sexual problem. Finally, he was not resistant to the notion of behavioral exercises, many of which involve masturbation.

The overall goal of Jim's therapy was for the therapist to act as a facilitator, an objective person who would regenerate his sexual confidence. Her eclectic background was useful in providing Jim with a foundation of explicit behavioral training combined with cognitive therapy. Following eclectic principles, the therapeutic plan for Jim operated at two levels. On a behavioral level, Jim received information about his anatomical functioning and his disorder. He also was given instruction in different practical exercises to increase his control over his sexual performance. On a cognitive/emotional level, the therapist treated Jim through biweekly psychotherapy sessions.

Like most men, Jim sought a rather short-term, limited treatment for his sexual problems. This is why he tried Viagra. He was disappointed that Viagra didn't work reliably. It surprised him to learn that medications like Viagra cannot work alone; there must also be sexual arousal and confidence for sexual behavior to proceed.

Therapy at first involved specific behavioral techniques and recommendations. Jim was taught the basic physiology of human sexual behavior, including a brief discussion of the four phases of the sexual response cycle. desire, excitement, orgasm, and resolution. The primary value of this education was to eliminate any myths Jim may have had regarding what to expect from sex. For example, most men are physiologically incapable of attaining an erection for a certain period immediately after ejaculation (the resolution phase). Unaware of this, many men become anxious because they are impotent because they can't orgasm repeatedly. Another example involved age. Although it is true that men remain sexually active throughout their lives, their ability to perform sexually does indeed decrease with age, usually becoming noticeable in the 40s or 50s. This age effect is compounded by illness, such as diabetes and hypertension. Simple information describing the physiology of the male sexual cycle will often dispel the anxieties associated with these myths.

Another topic of education involved the risk of contracting sexually transmitted diseases (STDs), particularly HIV, which was of particular concern given Jim's tendency to have unprotected sex. Jim was urged to practice using a condom, which the therapist described as "an acquired taste." She reassured him that although condoms were often distracting when first tried, their use quickly becomes routine, and that when used regularly, they have no significant impact on sexual performance.

Next, Jim was taught two specific techniques to improve his control over his erection (and thereby to improve his confidence in his sexual performance). Instructions for these techniques were given during early therapy sessions; he practiced these exercises at home.

The first of these is Seeman's exercise, also called The Start and Stop Technique. First, Jim was instructed to masturbate to orgasm quickly to reduce tension about achieving orgasm. The next time he masturbated, however, he was to gradually build up an erection and try to maintain it before ejaculating. Eventually Jim was able to attain an erection, maintain it for at least 3 minutes, let the erection slowly subside, and then to repeat the excitement, maintenance, and relaxation stages several times before finally reaching orgasm. The goals of this exercise are fourfold: (1) to develop control in attaining and maintaining an erection, (2) to increase the quality of the erection (i.e., its tumescence and duration), (3) to gain control over the timing of orgasm, and (4) to increase the patient's confidence in his sexual capabilities.

The second technique is known as the Kegel Exercise. In this exercise Jim was taught to tighten and loosen the pubococcygeal muscle (the muscle in the pelvis that restricts the flow of urine, sometimes called the "love muscle"). Jim flexed this muscle in two ways: by tightening and relaxing it for long durations and by rapidly flexing it for many repetitions. There were three general goals to this technique: (1) to increase muscle tone, (2) to stimulate the genital region, and (3) to increase the engorgement of blood into erectile tissue.

In addition to these physical exercises, Jim was also given specific instructions pertaining to his sexual activity. Most importantly, he was told to restrict the frequency of penetration so that he can concentrate his strength and thus make intercourse more exciting. In the therapist's words, "Intercourse is exhausting. You may want to think of other ways to have sex with your partner and save intercourse for the weekends." The therapist's second piece of advice was to delay penetration until both partners were ready. Often penetration will fail simply because the penis has not been sufficiently stimulated. Similarly, intercourse can be painful and/or uncomfortable for the partner if she is not sufficiently aroused. Intercourse is more pleasurable for both partners after sufficient foreplay.

Jim was very responsive to these suggestions. He came to therapy regularly and reported that he performed the exercises as instructed. As therapy progressed, the focus of the sessions gradually widened from his specific sexual problems to more introspective topics. A particularly important topic of discussion revolved around Jim's perceptions of the expectations of his partners. He stated that most of his partners seemed to focus almost exclusively on orgasm and that he felt a strong pressure to perform. He also complained that his sexual partners lacked any deep emotional involvement, which he felt diminished the quality of his sexual relationships with them. He wondered whether the stereotype of African American men as uncaring and macho may have contributed to this problem.

The therapist suggested that Jim's complaints may reveal more about himself than about others. For example, if Jim had a strong need for intimacy, why did he maintain his casual sexual relationships? Thus the focus of therapy gradually shifted from others' expectations to his own attitudes and beliefs. This widened the focus of therapy to deal with issues that did not relate directly to sex. They discussed his feelings about his acting career, his anxieties about his chances of forming satisfying romantic relationships, and his needs for intimacy, among other topics.

Acknowledging these underlying needs made him more confident in his relationships and more secure in his own worth.

Jim has been in therapy for about 6 months, and he seems to have made significant behavioral and emotional progress. After about two months of therapy Jim no longer complained about his erectile problems, and the behavioral aspects of his problem were for the most part resolved. After another month or so, he told the therapist that he found himself being less impulsive and casual about his sexual partners. By limiting his relationships to only those women in whom he had an emotional interest, he greatly increased his chances of developing an intimate and lasting relationship. In general, his emotional awareness is at a much more sophisticated level than it was when therapy began, and he is better able to assess his sexual and emotional needs and those of his partner. He also feels ready to commit to a long-standing, intimate relationship. At this point he is ready to discontinue therapy, but he agreed to return if problems arise.

PROGNOSIS

The prognosis for Jim is good. In general, a patient's prognosis in these sorts of cases is based on two factors: his responsiveness to therapy and his underlying emotional stability. To a large extent, patients who are willing to accept the therapist's suggestions and to perform the behavioral exercises generally show noticeable behavioral improvement after only one or two sessions. In addition, psychoeducation can prevent unrealistic anxieties and self-criticism.

Like Jim, many patients seeking therapy for sexual dysfunctions expect a direct, short-term behavioral therapy. When therapy begins to include broader issues, some become uncomfortable and either quit or switch to a more purely behavioral approach. Others, though, believe they can make gains from analysis and stay in therapy long after their behavioral symptoms disappear. The prevalence of ED increases dramatically with age, but, ironically, older men are generally more resistant to therapy. Perhaps because of their more traditional sexual upbringing, they are less willing to perform the different exercises, especially those involving masturbation. As a group, they also seem to be less self-aware and less amenable to self-discovery. It is possible that as sexual attitudes in society become more accepting, a growing cohort of men will be better able to face their sexual problems.

A major factor toward realizing this broader acceptance is the availability of medications like Viagra. Immediately upon its approval by the FDA, Viagra became a media sensation, which did much to medicalize ED and thus increase the public acceptance of treatment for this disorder. Celebrities, most notably politician Robert Dole and NASCAR driver Mark Martin agreed to appear in ads for Viagra, bringing the issue of sexual dysfunction further into the mainstream of American culture.

LOSING YOUR GRIP

Mathematician John Forbes Nash, Jr., winner of the 1994 Nobel Prize for Economics and famous subject of the book and movie *A Beautiful Mind*, suffered from Schizophrenia, Paranoid Type. In this form of schizophrenia, the person suffers from delusions involving grandiosity and persecution as well as vivid visual and auditory hallucinations. His disease robbed him of 30-odd productive years, and his case is both dramatic and tragic. This is a case perhaps less dramatic but certainly no less tragic, the case of a man suffering Schizophrenia, Residual Type, whose life has become a meaningless void

PRESENTING COMPLAINT

Jerry calmly attempted to walk across the German-Czech border on a road that led through the Bohemian Forest, not seeming to notice that this was a national boundary, or indeed even that it seemed highly unusual for someone to simply walk from one country another. German border guards detained him after he ignored their commands to stop and identify himself. The guards stated in their report that Jerry spoke in a vague and incoherent manner. He was calm, even passive, but he seemed to be completely unaware of where he was and the situation he had gotten himself into. He appeared to be an American around 50 years old, but this could not be confirmed because he carried no passport, travel visa, or any other identifying papers. In addition, he did not tell the guards anything specific about who he was or where he was from, saying only his name and that he was from "different places over there." He denied having any present address in Germany, any steady means of support, or any means of travel. Somewhat stupefied, the officers asked him just what he planned to do in the Czech Republic. Jerry replied, "Oh, just wander around, here and there. Nothing much, just see stuff, you know?"

Jerry was then taken to a U.S. Army hospital in Landstuhl, Germany for psychiatric observation. Here he was first diagnosed as schizophrenic and admitted. He was given chlorpromazine (Thorazine), an antipsychotic medication. Gradually he was now able to tell the hospital staff some basic information about his identity and background. He was 37 years old and lived with his parents, who had recently relocated to Munich, about 140 miles to the south. After five days on the ward Jerry seemed to be under control and was discharged to the custody of his parents, who reported that this was the third time Jerry had "wandered off" since he had moved to Munich the previous year. Although Jerry was somewhat stabilized, his parents were uncomfortable about having him stay in a foreign country and sent him to live near an aunt in Salt Lake City.

Jerry's aunt rented a small studio apartment for him and set him up with a job at a local supermarket. On his third day at the market, he walked off the job in the middle of his shift. Jerry returned to his apartment and did not go outside for several weeks; his aunt then became responsible for doing his laundry and shopping for his groceries. One morning at two o'clock, Jerry somehow became locked out of his apartment. He began yelling and banging at the door, and after about 20 minutes he finally broke it down and went inside. After this incident (which followed numerous other complaints by neighbors), Jerry's landlord began proceedings to evict him. Jerry's aunt promised to keep a closer eye on him and persuaded the landlord to hold off on the eviction. She then found him a part-time job as a church custodian. However, after two weeks of spotty attendance, Jerry again wandered off the job. This time, however, Jerry did not return to his apartment. After three days Jerry's aunt contacted the police and reported him missing.

Seven months later Jerry was arrested for vagrancy in a small town outside Bakersfield, California. The police contacted his parents, who returned to the United States to be present at his court hearing. A court-ordered psychiatric evaluation suggested that Jerry was not competent to stand trial. After consulting with his parents, the judge committed Jerry to a supervised group home run by a Veterans Administration hospital located near Los Angeles.

PERSONAL HISTORY

Jerry's descriptions of his past are for the most part extremely vague and lacking in content. He is unable to specify any dates, places, or events in his life. Occasionally he does provide some information, but most often this is inaccurate. For example, Jerry once reported to a hospital staff psychiatrist that he was an only child, when in fact he has an older brother. As a result, the hospital staff is forced to rely on other sources of information (his parents; his brother; his aunt; various medical, school, and military records) to provide the bulk of his background data. Although these secondary sources provided most of the basic information on the important events in Jerry's life, they could not describe his perceptions of these events or his emotional reactions to them. This subjective information is lost.

Jerry is the younger of two sons in an upper-middle-class family. His father is a successful executive for a German automobile manufacturer; his mother has never been employed outside the home. According to his family and the available records, his childhood was unremarkable. He seemed to have had a happy childhood and got along well with his family. He received good grades throughout school, mostly As and Bs. According to his parents, Jerry seemed to have had a successful social life in high school; he dated often and participated in football and track. After high school he enrolled at a large state university to study mechanical engineering. It is in college that his odd behavior first appeared.

Jerry's grades for his freshman year were considerably below his usual performance, averaging in the low C range. His professors, his roommate, and his neighbors in the dormitory

145

confirmed that he was not working up to his potential; they reported that he would frequently miss lectures and assignments. He seemed unconcerned about making friends or becoming active in campus activities, and his phone calls home became more infrequent as the year progressed. During his summer break he refused to work at a job set up by his father and spent most of his time either alone in his room or wandering aimlessly around the neighborhood. When he first returned home from college, Jerry's high school friends frequently came by to see him, but he seemed uninterested in them and made no effort to maintain their friendship. Although Jerry returned to college for the fall semester, it appears that he mostly just stayed in his dormitory room. His academic work continued to deteriorate, and he wound up failing every course. In addition to having academic difficulties, Jerry was beginning to cause serious problems in his dormitory. His roommate complained that he would spend almost all of his time in his room either sleeping or mumbling to himself. He did not do his laundry the entire semester, and he often went without bathing for stretches of up to 10 days. After eight weeks his roommate demanded to be transferred to another room. Over the winter break Jerry was informed that he would not be allowed to continue at the university because of his academic and social difficulties.

Four months after he left the university Jerry joined the Army. According to his evaluation during basic training, Jerry was found to be of above-average intelligence. However, his records also show that he lacked motivation and paid poor attention to instructions. He was described as a recruit who understood orders and instructions but followed them without any particular concern over what they were or if he would execute them properly. After completing basic training, Jerry was assigned to a clerical unit at a camp in Texas. Jerry's military record was similar to his record in boot camp. He never resisted orders, but he had to be supervised constantly to ensure that he actually carried them out. Finally he was discharged from the Army after his two-year hitch was completed.

After his discharge Jerry got a job working at a fast-food restaurant near Wichita Falls, Texas, but he left this job after about a month. Two weeks later he was arrested for shoplifting in Norman, Oklahoma. Apparently Jerry had attempted to walk off with several items from a grocery store. In light of his veteran status and his clean record, however, the storeowner decided not to press charges. For the next several years little was heard of Jerry, and his own accounts of this time are not particularly informative. Finally he was picked up for vagrancy and disorderly conduct in Omaha, Nebraska, after he repeatedly harassed passersby in a park, making strange and incoherent remarks such as shouting at a pile of garbage, "Use your common sense!" He was admitted to a local hospital for psychiatric observation. He was diagnosed as Schizophrenic, Paranoid Type and given haloperidol (Haldol), which reduced his more florid symptoms. Through Jerry's military records, the Omaha police managed to identify him and contact his parents in Germany. The court agreed to release Jerry to the care of his parents, and they took him to live with them in Munich.

CONCEPTUALIZATION AND TREATMENT

Jerry was 37 years old at admission, though he appeared to be 10 to 15 years older. Although his IQ was above average, his life seems to have had little meaning or coherence. He appeared to be unconcerned about the events of his life, and he showed little emotion in his day-to-day existence. He was not at all concerned by his lack of a permanent home, a steady job, companionship, or even a reasonably consistent source of food. He habitually withdrew from social situations, frequently wandering off from his home or job without any perceptible purpose. When he did engage in conversation, his speech was vague and lacking in content, as illustrated by his intake interview at the VA hospital:

> **Therapist:** Jerry, you left Salt Lake City about seven months ago, right?
> **Jerry:** Yeah, I guess.
> **Therapist:** So, what did you do during that time?

147

Jerry:	Oh, I don't know. Different things I guess.
Therapist:	Like what?
Jerry:	You know, this and that. Nothing special.
Therapist:	Well, like what? What did you do? Did you work?
Jerry:	Oh, well, I did odd jobs. You know.
Therapist:	What kind of odd jobs?
Jerry:	Little things here and there.
Therapist:	Like what? Can you think of any particular one?
Jerry:	Um, yeah. I was a janitor for a while.
Therapist:	How long did you do that?
Jerry:	Not long.
Therapist:	What's "not long"? A few days, weeks, months?
Jerry:	A few days, I guess.
Therapist:	Did you get paid for that?
Jerry:	No, I don't think so.
Therapist:	Well, how did you get money?
Jerry:	Different ways.
Therapist:	What kind of different ways?
Jerry:	You know, odd jobs and stuff.
Therapist:	Well, tell me this. How did you eat?
Jerry:	You know, garbage.

(Later)

Therapist:	Of all the places you were, where did you like it best?
Jerry:	Arizona, I guess.
Therapist:	Why Arizona?
Jerry:	Oh, different reasons.
Therapist:	Could you name one?
Jerry:	Well, it's drier there.
Therapist:	Do you mean it's less humid?
Jerry:	No, not really.
Therapist:	Well, what then?

Jerry: The ground's drier.
Therapist: What do you mean, "The ground is drier"?
Jerry: Well, there's less dew when you wake up.
Therapist: Oh, I see.

It is important to note that Jerry was not being secretive or evasive; he answered the questions as best he could, but his answers were strangely vague and distant.

Jerry's collection of social withdrawal, his blunted affect, his peculiar lack of motivation or initiative, his vague uninformative speech, his lack of any sense of planning or purpose, especially in the absence of any full-blown psychotic symptoms, characterizes someone suffering from Schizophrenia, Residual Type with prominent negative symptoms. Because his symptoms had existed more or less consistently for more than two years, his residual schizophrenia was categorized as continuous.

As is the case for most schizophrenics, Jerry's treatment was primarily pharmacological. Upon admission to the VA hospital, he was given Thorazine at a standard maintenance dosage of 100 milligrams four times a day. The primary purpose of this treatment was prophylactic: it was aimed at preventing a recurrence of an active phase of his disorder. Because Jerry's history included only isolated instances of psychotic behavior, his therapists were confident that this relatively low maintenance dose would be effective in warding off the reemergence of any future active phase. Patients who are presently in an active phase or who have a history of frequent decompensations generally are given higher doses.

In addition to taking medication, Jerry also participated in various therapeutic activities designed to improve his social and occupational skills. On Tuesdays and Fridays, the patients of Jerry's group home gathered together for community meetings. To promote their sense of control and responsibility, the patients were put in charge of these meetings. One patient was chosen to be the discussion leader, and another was chosen as the secretary who organized the proceedings and took minutes. These twice-weekly community meetings allowed the patients to raise issues and concerns in the presence of the entire ward and were intended to facilitate direct discussions among the patients and between the patients and staff. The primary focus of these discussions usually concerned practical issues on the ward (e.g., who was leaving or joining the ward, the policy on issuing day passes, information on field trips and events). The patients also participated in group therapy sessions. These sessions involved only a few patients at a time and were led by a single staff member. The object of these groups was to discuss interpersonal issues that are of concern to individual patients. The smaller size of these groups made it possible for an individual patient's problems to be addressed more thoroughly and in an open and frank manner.

Like most of the patients, Jerry was not particularly interested in participating in either group activity. After a few weeks on the ward, however, he was elected as the group secretary, an activity that had several positive, though indirect, effects. Mostly it forced him to interact with other patients just to organize the meetings. He also had to review the minutes of the last session prior to reading them, and he had to pay close attention during each meeting. Jerry's acceptance of these responsibilities was a positive sign.

A prime topic in group therapy was Jerry's indifference to social relationships. Jerry and his group leader set up a behavioral contract that reinforced him (mostly through public recognition and added privileges) for spending time interacting with other patients and staff members. Jerry responded to this contingency almost immediately. Instead of spending most of his recreation time alone, he began to take long walks around the hospital grounds with other patients. He also became much more involved in ward outings and other special events. For example, during an observation visit by a group of graduate students, Jerry approached several students to strike up conversations. Although he had a friendly attitude and was responsive to their questions, the students found the actual content of his speech to be rambling and rather uninformative. Nevertheless, even this limited approach behavior represented a big advance for Jerry.

Another aspect of Jerry's treatment program involved limited vocational training. As patients' symptoms begin to recede and become more manageable, they are enrolled in supervised workshops run by the hospital. Here they are trained to perform unskilled tasks (washing dishes, sorting cartons, etc.). Some patients are placed into semiskilled workshops. The therapeutic importance of this training is not in learning the vocational skills per se but rather in developing the discipline needed to hold a steady job. Jerry received carpentry training and presently works in the hospital's wood finishing shop, where patients refurbish used or abandoned furniture. This furniture is then used by the hospital or sold to the public.

The next step in the program is to move patients from the group home and set them up in semi-independent apartments, which are located in a complex about three miles from the hospital. Patients live in individual studio apartments and are responsible for their own food, laundry, transportation, and entertainment. The rent of the apartments is controlled, and the hospital can arrange to pay a patient's rent directly from his or her disability check if he or she proves to be incapable of doing so. In addition, the patients are supervised by a staff member who lives in the complex.

After three months in the group home, Jerry moved into his apartment. He works at the wood finishing shop three days a week and attends group therapy once a week. He has had no problems taking public buses to the hospital, and his attendance at work and at group therapy has remained around 90 percent. He seems to have no problem in performing his personal errands, such as shopping and doing his laundry. One month after moving into his apartment, Jerry's medication was reduced to 200 milligrams per day; for the past eight months he has been maintained on this relatively low dose and appears to be doing well. Jerry's only particularly noticeable symptom is his persistent disinterest in forming interpersonal relationships.

According to *DSM-IV*-TR, the term *schizophrenia* refers to a collection of diagnostic categories characterized by the presence of severe disturbances in thought, behavior, and interpersonal relationships. Researchers have organized schizophrenic behaviors into positive and negative symptoms. Positive symptoms refer to the most visible, odd psychotic manifestation of psychosis, such as hallucinations, delusions, and disorganized speech and behavior; negative symptoms refer to a relative lack of ordinary qualities such as emotional feeling, motivation, planning, and personal hygiene

When positive symptoms occur, they are usually expressed in episodes characterized by three distinct phases. During the *prodromal phase*, schizophrenics will show a significant deterioration of their social and cognitive functioning from their normal level, showing negative symptoms, mild positive symptoms, or most often both. For example, a schizophrenic might withdraw from social situations, neglect personal duties and hygiene, have strange thoughts and emotions, and lose energy and initiative. This deterioration in functioning, called "decompensation," is usually the first visible sign that a serious disorder is present. During the prodromal phase, other people generally describe schizophrenics as acting differently from their usual selves.

During the *active phase*, florid positive symptoms emerge. These include delusions (organized thought systems that are based on clearly false or bizarre ideas), hallucinations (vivid but false perceptions, such as hearing voices), disorganized thought patterns, odd speech, gross incoherence, inappropriate or restricted emotional reactions, and severe abnormalities of motor movement. *DSM-IV-TR* categorizes schizophrenics into five subtypes based on the constellation of symptoms they exhibit during this active phase of their disorder. These subtypes are described below.

As the positive symptoms recede, schizophrenics enter a *residual phase*. The symptoms of this phase are very similar to those in the prodromal phase with the exception that emotional blunting (lack of emotional reactivity) and neglecting one's duties are particularly pronounced in the residual phase. Other signs that could linger from the active phase are illogical thinking and some relatively mild delusions and hallucinations. The majority of schizophrenics display some symptoms for the rest of their lives; a complete absence of symptoms, known as *remission*, occurs in only about one third of the cases.

DSM-IV-TR distinguishes five subtypes of schizophrenia based on the particular pattern of positive symptoms exhibited during the active phase of the disorder. These five subtypes are labeled the catatonic type, disorganized type, paranoid type, undifferentiated type, and residual type. Jerry's behavior indicates residual type.

Schizophrenics categorized as *residual type* do not currently show the bizarre positive symptoms of an active phase. However, their behavior is characterized by negative symptoms such as disrupted daily functioning, social withdrawal, blunted affect, and illogical thinking. Most residual schizophrenics have a long-standing history of more or less continuous negative symptoms. In most cases there is evidence of a past active phase, and the diagnosis at that time may indicate a different subtype. Residual schizophrenics show relatively mildly strange characteristics, and their lives taken as a whole generally lack meaning and coherence. They seem to have a severe deficit in many of the higher-order abilities most people take for granted, such as setting life goals, making plans, and taking on and fulfilling responsibilities.

PROGNOSIS

On the whole, Jerry seemed to be functioning well in his structured job and sheltered living situation. Many of his more self-destructive negative symptoms, such as his inability to feed and clothe himself and his unwillingness to stay at a job, had decreased as he developed a more steady, normal routine. In all likelihood, though, Jerry will need to continue living in a fairly sheltered environment and taking his medication to maintain these therapeutic gains and prevent a recurrence of his more serious psychotic symptoms. As is the case with most chronic schizophrenics, getting Jerry to continue taking his medication is the key to his prognosis. Provided he remains in his supervised apartment and continues to take his antipsychotic medication, there is little reason to believe that Jerry's level of functioning will change significantly in the foreseeable future. Although his treatment had enabled him to live somewhat independently and even to be productive, there is little chance that Jerry will ever be able to live independently. Thus, his prognosis is poor, and the goal of treatment, like that of most schizophrenics, is not cure but continued maintenance.

Jerry received a comprehensive treatment that effectively combined pharmacological therapy and residential therapy. The vast majority of current treatment programs for schizophrenics cannot offer such facilities; most are short-term programs that can afford to treat only the most severely psychotic schizophrenics on a crisis management basis. Because of a lack of sheltered housing, patients whose overtly psychotic symptoms have subsided after a brief period, sometimes as short as a few days, are simply released. In many cases these schizophrenics have no steady home or family, and they just wander the streets until their next active phase emerges. For most schizophrenics, this revolving door syndrome will be a behavior pattern that will predominate the rest of their lives.

_____

WHY CAN'T I SLEEP?

_____

PRESENTING COMPLAINT

2:00 a.m. Once again Bill couldn't sleep. He just stared at the ceiling thinking about how tired he was going to be tomorrow. He'd be wasted for that big presentation, and he just *had* to get some sleep. He was scared about screwing up. He knew that when he didn't sleep, his mind was dull, he looked bored, and he couldn't respond to questions with any confidence or style. He could just see it, him standing up there during his presentation, stammering to try to find the word he wanted. It was going to be terrible!

3:15 a.m. Why didn't the sleeping pill work? His internist had prescribed zolpidem (Ambien) for sleep. It seemed to work for a couple of hours, but by 2:00 or 3:00 he'd be wide awake again. Once he tried taking a second one at about this time, but he felt like he was in a fog the rest of the day. Never again! He really couldn't afford that tomorrow. Alcohol didn't work either. A few drinks before bed usually put him to sleep, but he'd be up in the middle of the night, just like when he took the Ambien, only he felt crummier the next day. He tried mixing Ambien and alcohol. Once. It was worse than taking a second pill. He tried antihistamines, melatonin, and nighttime cold medications. Nothing helped his sleep.

4:05 a.m. This has been going on how long now? At least a couple of months, maybe longer. He went to the sleep center at the local hospital a couple weeks ago and had hoped that they would give him some answers. But as far as he could tell from what the neurologist said, they really couldn't find any conclusive reason for his insomnia. A whole night and then a whole day at the place with all those wires glued to his head, you'd think they'd find something!

155

Case 15

All they said was that they were referring him to a psychologist. A psychologist? Was it all in his head? His appointment was this afternoon, after the presentation. What the hell, maybe he would go and talk about getting fired . . .

5:10 a.m. He was getting angry now, as he usually did when he couldn't sleep all night. There was Jenny, sleeping soundly next to him. He could hit her! She didn't have any big meeting tomorrow, why couldn't they switch places: she could stay up and let him sleep! Why couldn't he just get some sleep, just once? Why tonight? There was so much riding on tomorrow's presentation . . .

Suddenly the alarm clock rang. 6:15 a.m. Bill was groggy, sore, and exhausted. His arms and legs felt like lead, and he wanted to sleep for a week. Sure, now he falls asleep! For what, an hour? He dragged himself out of bed, stumbled through his routine of getting ready for work, and drove off to certain death at the presentation . . .

PERSONAL HISTORY

Bill didn't die that morning, but he looked pretty beat up when he saw the psychologist at 3:00 that afternoon. His face was lined and worried, and he was mildly agitated. But the therapist noted that his eyes were not particularly sunken or puffy, and although he had slight bags under his eyes, he did not have the dark rings common after prolonged sleep deprivation. In short, he clearly felt frustrated and desperate to get more sleep, but he really didn't look like a man who hadn't slept well in months.

Bill's personal history provided few clues to explain his insomnia. He was a 54-year-old married father of two children, a married daughter and a son in college. He has been married for 27 years and reports no problems at home, other than envy at his wife's sound sleep. He earned a BA and MBA from the University of Missouri and is the director of marketing for a large packaging manufacturer based in St. Louis.

156

He could not think of anything remarkable about his childhood. He grew up in a small farm town in northern Missouri, where his father owned a feed supply business. His parents were married until his father died about five years ago. He maintains a "friendly but not especially close" relationship with his two older sisters. He denies any abuse or traumatic event while growing up. His childhood sleeping patterns were typical: a few isolated episodes of bedwetting, nightmares, and sleeplessness, but nothing unusual. His adult sleep history was also relatively ordinary. Every so often there were times when he had trouble falling asleep, but nothing like what he was experiencing over the past few months.

He denied any personal history of psychological problems. Family history was significant for a paternal grandfather who probably had problems with alcohol but was never treated. Also, his mother was a little nervous and demanding, but again there was no history of any formal treatment. When asked to elaborate on this, he noted that his mother had become much more anxious and dependent since his father passed away. Now she would call him every night at 11:30 when he was home. He found this annoying but didn't have the heart to tell her to stop.

Current habits were described as occasional social alcohol use, but nothing excessive: no history of abuse, no DUIs, etc. He quit smoking about ten years ago. Caffeine use was usually 2 cups of coffee in the morning and another cup or a soda in the afternoon. Lately, though, he had increased his caffeine intake to three to four cups of coffee every morning plus another two cups or sodas in the afternoon. He used to have a cup of coffee after dinner, but he switched to decaf about a month ago upon the suggestion of his doctor.

His sleep habits were described as getting up at 6:15 every workday. On weekends he got up later, sometimes as late as 10:00. His bedtime was 11:30, after the news, but usually he was so exhausted when he got home from work that he fell asleep on the couch in the early evening. But for some reason when he went to bed later, he couldn't sleep. He wondered if there was something about his bedroom or sleeping with Jenny that kept him awake, and

157

he had tried sleeping on the couch or in one of the children's rooms, but without any noticeable improvement.

CONCEPTUALIZATION AND TREATMENT

Anyone who treats insomnia must first have a good working knowledge of the basic elements and patterns of sleep, what sleep researchers call *sleep architecture*. In brief, sleep is divided into two fundamental states: REM and NREM (pronounced "remm" and "non-remm," respectively). REM sleep is also called paradoxical sleep because the brain is active with brainwaves similar to the waking state, but the body is deeply relaxed because of a massive inhibition of voluntary muscles. REM is when most dreaming takes place. NREM sleep has 4 stages, which are simply called Stage 1, 2, 3, and 4. These four stages are defined by changes in brainwaves; sleep gets progressively deeper as the sleeper progresses from Stage 1 to Stage 4.

When a person falls asleep, he or she enters Stage 1, a light sleep. The person will then take anywhere from 50 to 110 minutes to progress through Stages 2, 3, and 4. Then the person quickly returns through Stages 3, 2, and 1 before beginning a period of REM sleep, which usually lasts around 15 to 30 minutes. Then the NREM-REM cycle repeats three, four, or five times a night. As people get older, their sleep architecture tends to break down. Furthermore they get less deep NREM sleep and awaken more frequently during the night.

At the sleep lab Bill was given the usual protocol of a polysomnogram (PSG, an all-night test that records brainwaves, muscle tone, and breathing during sleep) and a multiple sleep latency test (MSLT, a test that monitors brainwaves during a series of opportunities to nap at four times during the day). What Bill's tests did show were a relatively long sleep latency (it took him about 62 minutes to fall asleep), a short sleep duration (his total sleep time was 293 minutes), and mild excessive daytime sleepiness, especially in the late afternoon (Stage 1 sleep began after 17 minutes at 1:00 p.m. and 8 minutes at 3:00 p.m.). This is less sleep than is usual for most people, but it is not unusual for the first night in a novel sleep environment, something sleep clinicians call a "first night effect." Most significantly, Bill's record contained a note of "subjective insomnia." In the morning when the sleep technician asked him how he slept, he estimated that he was asleep for less than an hour. Although getting slightly less than five hours of sleep is well below average, it is much more than "hardly any at all." Bill believes he is getting less sleep than he actually does.

Bill's sleep tests were significant for what they *didn't* show as well as for what they showed. In general, his sleep architecture was roughly normal for someone his age. Measures of his breathing (chest expansion, oxygen saturation, carbon dioxide saturation) did not indicate any significant sleep apnea, a relatively common problem involving the periodic disruption of breathing during sleep. His MSLT did not include any indication of deep sleep (Stages 3 and 4) or REM sleep, which are indications of narcolepsy, a condition where the person is plagued by sudden sleep attacks. Poor sleeping at night combined with excessive daytime sleeping is a pattern that may indicate a circadian rhythm sleep disorder—a condition where the person falls asleep too late and wakes up too late. His sleep results did not suggest this problem. All told, these indications rule out most sleep disorders, leaving a diagnosis of Primary Insomnia.

Bill's treatment was organized into three parts. First, the psychologist would provide education about sleep so that Bill could gain a better understanding of his condition and gain reassurance that his sleep patterns are roughly normal. Then would come the primary focus of treatment, which would be to develop better sleep hygiene, a set of behaviors and habits that promote good sleep. A final goal was to investigate any work stress or family problems that might be keeping Bill awake.

Being intelligent and open to information, Bill readily understood the concepts behind sleep physiology and sleep architecture. He was shocked that he had actually slept almost five hours during his night in the lab. Many patients with subjective insomnia argue with the test results, but fortunately Bill accepted his reported sleep duration as a medical fact and tried to learn from it. Having the patient gain a basic understanding sleep is an important first step toward motivating the person to accept and implement the changes required to improve sleep hygiene.

Bill's therapist worked to improve his sleep hygiene through a variety of suggestions. The first group examined Bill's sleep environment. In general, Bill had a good sleep environment. He slept in a comfortable bed in a dark, quiet room where interruptions are very rare. There was a TV set, but it was turned off at bedtime. Two other appliances did cause problems, however. One was Bill's clock. The therapist's first suggestion to Bill was a very simple one: to turn his clock so he couldn't see it from his bed. Bill's therapist explained that it is normal to wake up briefly a few times throughout the night. However, when Bill looked at his clock and saw that one more hour had elapsed, he assumed that he hadn't slept between his glances at the clock, whereas he probably had been asleep for most or all of that time. If he couldn't see the clock, then this anxiety-provoking clock watching would stop. The other problem was the phone. Bill's almost nightly calls from his mother appeared to upset him. The therapist suggested that Bill talk to his mother using another phone so that his feelings of being upset did not become linked to the bedroom environment. To make his sleep environment as conducive to sleep as possible, the therapist instructed Bill to practice a relaxation technique in bed every night before sleep. In Bill's case, this took the form of progressive muscle relaxation, a routine involving (1) breathing deeply and slowly, (2) focusing his mind on a relaxing, pleasant thought, and (3) gently tensing and relaxing muscle groups from head to toe and visualizing his tension draining out of his body into the bed.

A second group of suggestions dealt with Bill's sleep habits. When Bill can't sleep, he tends to lie in his bed and stare at his bedroom ceiling, all the while becoming more and more anxious and frustrated as the night wears on. Bill was urged to move to a different room when he can't sleep, and to return to his bed only when he felt sleepy. In Bill's case, this involved getting out of bed and moving to the family room. There he would relax by watching TV, reading, and having a light snack. If something was bothering him, he could address that problem (for example, make a list of points to cover in his presentation) so it wouldn't keep nagging at him. The important idea here is that by staying in bed when he can't sleep, Bill is developing a learned association between his bedroom and his anxiety and frustration. Another habit the therapist wanted to change was Bill's nightly phone call from his mother. This obviously upset him, which of course did not leave him in the best condition to fall asleep. The therapist urged Bill to talk to his mother less, ideally once or twice a week, and certainly not just before bed.

A third topic of therapy concerned Bill's sleep schedule. It may seem ironic that one of the best ways to promote sleep is to instruct patients to sleep *less* through a technique called sleep restriction. It's not really having them sleep loss, it's more having them not sleep at the wrong times. Thus, Bill was instructed to avoid his evening naps and to maintain his normal sleep and waking times, even on Saturdays and Sundays. Although it was understandable that Bill would want to nap after work and sleep in on weekends, these habits actually weakened his sleep architecture. As much as possible, it is best to concentrate sleep into a single period at night and avoid sleep at other times.

A fourth area of concern involved Bill's lifestyle. One problem people often have is heavy eating or drinking shortly before dinner. Bill did not eat before trying to sleep, and he found from experience that drinking alcohol didn't work. Alcohol tends to promote falling asleep, but it disrupts the underlying sleep architecture and thus results in a more disrupted and less deep sleep. Bill also avoided caffeine after 3:00 p.m.; his therapist reinforced this but suggested eliminating caffeine after noon, just to make sure. Perhaps one of the most important lifestyle factors that affects sleep is exercise. Although heavy exercise should be avoided within three hours or so of bedtime (when the body is still coming down from its physical stimulation), it is important to exercise regularly to promote good sleep. This helps work off stress and frustration and develops a physical need for restorative sleep. In our hectic society full of mechanical conveniences, most people do not get adequate exercise, and Bill was no exception.

Another area of concern involved medications. Bill was instructed to reduce and eventually eliminate his use of sleeping aids, after consulting with his doctor. In general, sleep medications are intended as short-term aids that should be used only occasionally and not continuously for more than one or two weeks. By taking Ambien nightly, Bill was developing a psychological and physical dependency on his medication to sleep, making attempts to sleep without it much more difficult. This phenomenon is called a rebound effect and must be considered whenever medications are involved to promote sleep.

Finally, Bill's therapists looked beyond his sleep problems and gently probed possible psychological or situational factors that may be contributing to his insomnia. There are many complex relationships between psychological problems and sleep, but as a general rule, people with anxiety tend to have problems falling asleep, whereas those with depression often find it hard to remain asleep. In Bill's case, the sources of his anxiety presented clearly at his initial evaluation: stress over his work and guilt over his mother. Brief cognitive therapy addressed these issues in an attempt to reduce their tendency to contribute to his insomnia.

PROGNOSIS

Insomnia cases involve a mixed group of problems. In some cases, behavioral habits and lifestyles contribute significantly to the inability to fall asleep, and in these cases relatively brief treatment focusing on psychoeducation and behavior modification can be very effective. Bill was a motivated patient who was open to the therapist's many suggestions. He is likely to show relatively quick and (for him at least) dramatic improvement.

Many cases of insomnia are not so clear-cut, however. In most cases, there is an underlying psychological problem that must first be addressed and treated before any real progress can be made. Typically these patients are not open to psychological explanations for their problems, preferring to see themselves as suffering from a medical problem rather than a mental one. They tend to resist therapy and to be noncompliant with behavioral suggestions.

It should not be forgotten that often insomnia is the manifestation of a physical illness, ranging anywhere from chronic pain to medication side effects to hyperthyroidism to specific sleep problems such as restless legs syndrome (RLS). For this reason, it is critical that insomniacs receive thorough medical evaluations, including sleep studies if warranted. There may be more at stake than just a getting good night's sleep.

A FADING MEMORY

At the time of this writing, Ronald Reagan, fortieth President of the United States, lives away from the public eye in California. Several years ago, his wife, Nancy, disclosed publicly that the former president has been suffering from Dementia of the Alzheimer's Type, commonly called Alzheimer's disease. Although few details of his treatment have been made public, the following case may provide a sense of what he and his family have been experiencing.

PRESENTING COMPLAINT

Emma is a 74-year-old woman who lives alone in a small town in central Indiana. She has been widowed for six years. Her daughter and son-in-law, Susan and Bill, also live in this town and visit her several times a week.

Approximately two months ago Emma and Susan went on a shopping trip to Indianapolis. Emma seemed to enjoy the ride to the city, and she and Susan engaged in a friendly, although somewhat vacuous and disorganized, conversation. When they arrived downtown, Emma became very confused. She did not know where she was or why she was there. She asked several odd questions, such as "What's the name of this place?" and "Why are you taking me here?" She became very upset and asked her daughter to take her home again. Susan was used to her mother being befuddled now and then, but she had never seen her this disoriented. When she tried to explain where they were and the purpose of the trip, Emma continued to be confused and agitated. Seeing little use in continuing the outing, Susan drove home.

When they returned to Emma's house, Susan noticed other signs that something was wrong with her mother. Emma had left her stove on, and she had also left a pan with scrambled eggs in the refrigerator. Emma could not say how long the stove had been on or when she had put the pan in the refrigerator; in fact, she had no memory of having made scrambled eggs at all. She soon became very upset, refused to answer any more questions, and demanded that Susan leave.

That evening Susan called to check up on her mother and ask if she were feeling ill. Emma denied having any problems and asked Susan why in the world she might have thought so. Emma had only a vague memory of their trip that morning and no recollection whatsoever of their argument.

The next day Susan took Emma to see their family physician. He found nothing wrong with her physically, but he did notice that she was vague, even evasive, about recent events. Alerted by Susan's concerns, he administered the Mini Mental Status Exam (MMSE, Folstein, Folstein, & McHugh, 1975) and found that Emma suffered memory loss, mild disorientation, and difficulty following instructions. He then referred her for a more detailed neuropsychological examination at the neurology clinic of a nearby hospital. Emma was given a battery of diagnostic tests, including a CAT (computed axial tomography) scan, an EEG (electroencephalogram), and various blood tests. After analyzing the results of these tests, the neurologist found what he expected: evidence of cortical atrophy and nonspecific, bilateral brainwave slowing. He was noncommittal about his diagnosis, but he mentioned the possibility of Alzheimer's disease. Susan and Bill were dissatisfied with this diagnosis and sought a second opinion. They were referred to the neurology clinic of a major teaching hospital in Indianapolis.

PERSONAL HISTORY

Susan and Bill drove Emma to the neurology clinic in Indianapolis. Emma appeared nervous, confused, and disoriented during the initial interview with the neurology resident; it was left to Susan to provide the bulk of Emma's history.

Emma was born in Chicago, the daughter of Swedish immigrants. She was the second child of six. She had an eighth-grade education and worked as a store clerk in Chicago until her marriage at age 22. Susan was born two years later; medical complications during the birth prevented her from having any more children. Soon afterward Emma's husband bought a hardware store in central Indiana and moved the family. When Emma was 40 years old, she took a job as a teller at a local bank. She retired when she was 65. Four years ago she was widowed.

Emma's medical history is unremarkable. She is described by her daughter as a "light social drinker." When she was first married, she smoked tobacco occasionally, but she then quit and has not smoked in over 40 years. She has no history of any head injury, thyroid disease, or any other serious medical problem. Fifteen years ago she had cataract surgery without any complications.

The medical history of Emma's family of origin is somewhat unclear. Her mother died about 20 years ago at the age of 81, and her father died over 50 years ago when Emma was still a teenager. Susan cannot state the cause of their deaths other than saying that Emma's mother died of old age. One of Emma's brothers was diagnosed as having Alzheimer's disease before he passed away four years ago; her other siblings are still alive and in reasonably good health.

According to Susan, Emma suffers from "minor mood problems" involving occasional feelings of anxiety and depression. Fifteen months ago Emma was prescribed the SSRI antidepressant sertraline (Zoloft), and she continues to take a low dose of 50 milligrams per day. Other than this, Emma has no history of any psychiatric disorder. Unusually for someone her age, she takes no other medication.

When the neurologist asked Susan to describe Emma's "minor mood problems" in more detail, she replied:

> Mom was fine until a couple of years ago. She had been living alone for about four years. She seemed okay at first, but after a while she started staying home a lot. She didn't seem to want to go out much, even to visit friends, and she started calling us less often. She seemed to get angry and irritable with other people much easier than she used to. She also starting getting confused about things—where she kept different things around the house and who she talked to, that sort of thing. This was all pretty gradual. Lately she's been very hesitant to do things on her own. It seems that I take her just about everywhere now: shopping, to the beauty parlor, to the bank. And you know about the trip to Indianapolis.
>
> About a year ago we took her to a gerontology specialist. We told him what we had been noticing, but he didn't seem to think that she was unusual. He gave her medication for her anxiety, though. She still takes it, but it doesn't seem to help much; actually she seems to be getting worse. As you know, we saw another neurologist two weeks ago, but he also didn't seem to know what was wrong.

CONCEPTUALIZATION AND TREATMENT

Emma's worsening memory and increasingly frequent periods of disorientation suggest that she is suffering from a progressive dementia. According to *DSM-IV-TR*, dementia is a condition marked by a significant memory loss as well as problems in at least one of the following: aphasia (disruptions in the ability to use or understand language), agnosia (inability to recognize familiar objects or events), apraxia (difficulty in carrying out coordinated actions), or executive functioning (disorientation in familiar settings, poor concentration, impaired judgment, concrete thinking, irritability, and aggressiveness). In some cases there may be evidence of paranoid delusions and hallucinations

Several neuropsychological tests have been developed to measure the extent of a person's dementia; the MMSE is perhaps the most commonly used. This is a brief in-office test administered by the physician that tests orientation, memory, perception, and the ability to follow simple instructions. Her score was 14 out of 30. She was able to state her name, but she did not know the correct date, the day of the week, or the month. She could not say where she was, or even that she was in a hospital. She was able to repeat a list of three words, but she could not recall these words five minutes later, nor did she remember that they had been given to her at all. She was also unable to count backward. She could follow simple commands, but became confused at complicated three-step instructions. Her ability to draw a figure and write a simple sentence was intact. These responses indicate moderate to severe impairment in her cognitive abilities. This finding is not wholly surprising, considering Susan's description of her odd behavior. Another factor consistent with this result is her age. Whereas dementia is rare for persons under 50, the prevalence of this disorder increases greatly with age.

About half of all cases of dementia are diagnosed as Alzheimer's disease. This form of dementia is marked by an insidious onset and a gradual but inexorable deterioration in a multitude of intellectual abilities. Memory, judgment, and decision-making processes are affected, and personality changes might be evident. Agitation and irritability are common, and paranoid delusions and hallucinations could be present. Patients experience difficulty in comprehending complex and abstract problems, and over time the ability to perform even simple tasks becomes impaired. Eventually the patients are no longer able to care for themselves.

There is no practical test to provide a definitive diagnosis of Alzheimer's disease; the only conclusive evidence is the existence of senile plaques and neurofibrillary bundles in brain tissue. Unfortunately, these can be detected only by brain biopsy, which is usually conducted at autopsy. (Brain biopsy has been used for premorbid diagnosis of Alzheimer's disease, but only in extraordinary cases where there is a good possibility of finding another potentially treatable cause of dementia, such as brain tumor or stroke.) Without a reliable positive indicator, a diagnosis is made when other known causes of dementia are ruled out. When symptoms manifest themselves before age 65, the disorder is said to have an early onset; symptoms that emerge after age 65 indicate a late onset. Emma's symptoms and test results led the neurology resident who interviewed her to conclude that the chances were about 90 percent that she suffered from Alzheimer's disease. The attending neurologist, a specialist in research on dementia, concurred with this assessment.

Emma was prescribed donepezil (Aricept), which works to increase the availability of acetylcholine (Ach), a neurotransmitter involved in memory and cognition. In the short term these drugs may improve cognitive functioning to some degree, but in the long term they work to retard the progression of the disease. Nevertheless, this provides significant lifestyle benefits.

Even with the advent of these medications, the bulk of therapy typically focuses not on the demented patients themselves but on the caregivers, usually family members, who must now deal with the profound burden of caring for them. The need for this therapy should not be underestimated. First, it can inform the patients and their families what the disease is and what they can expect in terms of functioning. Second, this therapy can suggest several strategies to aid patients' memory and concentration, thus prolonging their ability to function independently. Third, this therapy gives both the patients and their families a place to air frustrations and complaints. Last, and perhaps most important, this therapy helps the patients—and especially their caregivers—to cope with the relentless progression of this disorder.

Immediately after Emma's diagnosis, she and Susan began meeting weekly with a counselor from the local hospital. Gradually these meetings became less frequent until they were held approximately once a month. These sessions provided both Emma and Susan with an empathic listener with whom they could share their doubts, fears, and frustrations.

The counselor also provided patient and caregiver with some specific behavioral strategies to help them cope with Emma's impaired memory and judgment. First, the counselor suggested that when other people ask Emma questions, they should ask recognition questions rather than recall questions. For example, Emma found it easier to answer, "Did you have eggs or cereal for breakfast?" instead of "What did you have for breakfast?" Similarly, "Was that Gladys on the phone?" was easier to answer than "Who was that on the phone?"

A second set of tricks was designed to reduce Emma's increasing confusion. One trick was put labels around the house. Labels near the door reminded her to lock the door and to turn off the stove. Because Emma forgot which light switches controlled which lights, Susan labeled each switch with its corresponding fixture: Hall Light, Kitchen Light, Porch Light, and so on. As Emma's aphasia worsened, she gradually lost her ability to recognize the words on these labels. At this point Susan, with a fair amount of ingenuity, added pictures to many of the labels.

Finally, because Emma often lost her place in the middle of doing her chores or errands, Susan wrote out directions for various everyday tasks. For instance, the particular steps involved in doing the laundry were written out in detail and attached to the washing machine. Emma found it easier to complete these tasks if she had some concrete set of directions to refer to when she forgot her place in the sequence of steps.

An important aspect of counseling is to provide reassurance and encouragement to the families of Alzheimer patients, who often need this help as much as the patients themselves. One issue that emerges early is simply trying to accept the disease. One indication of her denial was the great discrepancy between her description of her mother's behaviors and Emma's performance on neuropsychological tests. Susan reported that Emma suffered from "getting confused" and had "minor mood problems." In contrast,

Emma's MMSE score of 14 provides evidence of considerable cognitive impairment. Another indication of Susan's denial was her rejection of the findings of Emma's first neurological examination. Ronald Reagan's public announcement of his own diagnosis of Alzheimer's disease has served as a model for openness and allowed many patients and family members to overcome their own resistance.

Once she finally accepted the diagnosis of Alzheimer's disease, Susan was able to care for her mother in a more constructive way. Much of her frustration at Emma's seemingly illogical behaviors evaporated. She became more aware of the many signs of her mother's dementia, and she became more patient and caring. She was eager to set up the various memory tricks around Emma's home. She also made an effort to explain Emma's condition to friends, who had been surprised by the mother's apathetic and sometimes hostile attitude. She decided to take over Emma's financial affairs as well.

As Emma became more impaired, Susan found it increasingly difficult to meet the demands of herself and her family while looking after the constant needs of her mother. She felt almost constant feelings of frustration and resentment, as well as pangs of guilt. Counseling for Susan was particularly important now. She was urged not to let her mother's needs rob her of her own life. When Emma's cognition degenerated to the point where constant care was necessary, Susan was encouraged to accept this fact and either hire a private nurse or companion or place Emma in a nursing home. Institutionalizing her mother was the most difficult decision Susan ever had to make; supportive therapy aided her and her family in coming to grips with this painful issue.

PROGNOSIS

Six months after her visit to the clinic in Indianapolis, Emma was unable to recall the majority of recent events, most noticeably conversations she had had with her family or friends. She was frequently disoriented and increasingly had great difficulty linking individual actions into purposeful behaviors. One by one she gave up her friendships (usually because she failed even to recognize her friends and acquaintances), and she gradually became more irritable around her daughter.

After a year she was brought back to the specialist in Indianapolis and given a follow-up examination. As he predicted, her deterioration was marked. She now scored a 5 on the MMSE and did not appear to understand most questions.

After another year her cognitive functioning had deteriorated to the point where she was unable to care for herself. She could no longer dress or wash herself and was frequently incontinent. At this point, Susan was spending virtually all her time at her mother's home. With the encouragement of her husband and her counselor, Susan finally decided to place Emma in a nursing home. There Emma's cognitive abilities continued to deteriorate, and she died of pneumonia approximately 18 months later.

The course of Emma's disease was fairly typical. The progression of Alzheimer's disease is extremely variable, from only a few months to over ten years. Furthermore, it is rare that patients with Alzheimer's disease die as a direct result of their dementia; however, their prolonged illness makes them especially vulnerable to opportunistic diseases such as pneumonia that ordinarily would not be fatal. Perhaps most typical of all was the fact that Emma's treatment was as much for her caregiver daughter and her family as for herself.

DIRTY FOOD

PRESENTING COMPLAINT

Jill is a 25-year-old single woman who works as a flight attendant for a major airline. After getting home late at night after a particularly difficult flight, Jill went out to a local convenience store and bought a half-gallon of chocolate ice cream, a 1-pound box of cookies, a medium-sized frozen pizza, a loaf of French bread, and a quart of milk. When she got home, she put the pizza in the oven and waited impatiently for it to cook; everything else stayed on the table. She took the pizza out five minutes early, when it was just edible, and placed it with the other food. She then lunged into the food and ate everything she bought as quickly as she could, stuffing in huge mouthfuls and dribbling milk, crumbs, and pizza sauce down her chin and onto her blouse. When she felt like she would burst, she ran to the bathroom, knelt in front of the toilet, thrust her hand down her throat, and vomited everything she had just eaten.

The next day Jill consulted an internist for help concerning recent periods of weakness and dizziness, the most recent of which occurred on yesterday's flight. After performing a routine examination, he asked her about her eating habits. Jill was surprised; she had forgotten about last night's binge and didn't connect her eating habits with her symptoms. Although she was extremely embarrassed and felt guilty about describing these to him, she felt that if she wanted to get well, she had to tell the truth. She confessed to a long-standing pattern of binge eating and followed by purging through vomiting. This binge-purge pattern began years ago, but it has become more severe and more frequent since Jill began working as a flight attendant. She described last night's binge and purge in detail. According to Jill, this was a fairly typical amount of food for a binge, which she usually finishes within 20 minutes. She almost always induces vomiting right after binge eating. At first she stuck her finger down her throat, but gradually that became less effective. Now she usually purges by sticking her hand down her throat, though on occasion she has used other objects, including a Popcicle stick, a spoon, and a folded electric cord.

Jill acknowledged that her eating behavior must appear very strange and repulsive to him; it was certainly disgusting to her. She promised herself a thousand times that she'd stop, but she couldn't. She goes through this binge-purge cycle once or twice a day when she is at home; she can control herself to some extent on the road and only rarely binges when she is traveling. She estimates that she binges an average of five to six times per week. She also swallows a "handful" of laxatives, perhaps 12 to 15, once or twice a week. In addition, she takes Lasix (a diuretic) and diet pills in an effort to lose weight.

Although it was very difficult for Jill to tell her doctor about her strange eating patterns, she felt relieved once she did. Her doctor reassured her that she wasn't disgusting. Instead he sympathetically explained that it sounded like she had bulimia nervosa, which is not so uncommon in young women, and referred her to an eating disorders clinic. Before her appointment at the clinic, Jill read several articles about this disorder and was very relieved to find out that, as her internist had said, many other women suffered from these same odd symptoms. When her therapist first met her and asked her what brought her to the eating disorders clinic, she looked down and replied, "I have bulimia."

PERSONAL HISTORY

Jill is the youngest of three daughters in what she considers to be a fairly average middle-class family. When asked if her parents had any psychological or medical problems, she described her father as having "some problems with alcohol, but I wouldn't call him an alcoholic." Her mother seemed to have had occasional episodes of depression. So far as Jill knew, neither parent ever sought professional help. Jill was aware of some degree of conflict between her parents, but she did not feel they were unusual in this regard. She denied any history of abuse or neglect.

Jill described herself as having been preoccupied with her weight since she was 13 years old and having been constantly concerned about being thin ever since. At age 14 she reached her adult height of 5 feet 6 inches and weighed 130 pounds, which she considered to be very overweight. She dieted on and off for the next two years, but without any lasting success. When she was 16, a friend told her about self-induced vomiting. Initially she was horrified at this idea, but nevertheless she tried this method after she overate one night. She found that the vomiting was tolerable, and she quickly adopted this method as a clever trick to diet without being hungry. She remembers thinking, "Throwing up isn't so bad; it sure beats starving." During the next year she lost over 20 pounds.

When Jill was 17, she weighed 105 pounds and felt more or less satisfied with her weight. She decided to apply for a job as a model. The modeling agency did not hire her, saying that she should try to lose some weight. Discouraged, Jill gave up on modeling and, with the encouragement of her parents, enrolled in a local private university.

In college Jill had more freedom to experiment with her eating habits. She discovered that by vomiting she could eat rather large amounts of food and still maintain her weight. Gradually her binge eating became more severe and more frequent until she was eating huge amounts of food twice daily. She would build up a little stash of food no one else could eat, which she called this her "dirty food." It was now becoming more and more difficult to hide this stash, as well as her odd eating behavior, from her roommates. Sometimes she even stole food from them. Jill recalled one particularly embarrassing incident:

Shelley had bought a bunch of ice cream and potato chips for a party for a club she was in. Well, I couldn't stand having all that stuff around, so I just went at it. Of course I had planned to replace it all, but I didn't get around to it before she got back. Boy, was she shocked to find all that stuff gone! I felt really bad and apologized. I made up a story about how some of my friends came over and we all couldn't resist it. She didn't say anything, but I think she knew what really happened.

At this time Jill also began abusing laxatives and diuretics. Jill's excessive and impulsive habits branched out to alcohol as well. She smoked a little marijuana but never really did any other drugs; mostly she drank. A lot. She started going to lots of parties, and she became intoxicated and vomited at almost every one. Sometimes she had casual sex during these parties, but not often. Now that she thinks about it, her frequent vomiting probably limited that. By her junior year she began to feel weak and ill for long stretches, and she started missing class assignments. She also began staying away from her friends on campus, partly because she felt so embarrassed and ashamed about her eating. During her junior year Jill dropped out of college and worked as a receptionist. Relieved of the social pressures of campus life, she gradually decreased her binge eating to an average of twice a week over the next few years, and gradually her weight increased to 135 pounds. Jill felt totally disgusted with herself at this time of her life. She remembers feeling pretty depressed and hopeless around then, but she never saw anyone about it. Upon the recommendation of a friend, she decided to make a change in her life and enrolled in flight attendant school.

Jill was surprised to find that the airline had a strict weight limit for their flight attendants. Trainees who were overweight were dropped from the program, and attendants who did not make their weight target were grounded. Worried that she would be cut from the program, Jill now became more weight-conscious than ever. She frantically sought ways to lose weight, and she began binge eating and purging two or three times daily. She eliminated alcohol from her diet and ate only dietary foods (vegetables, diet soda, and so forth) when she was not binge eating. After two months she had lost 20 pounds. She was now within the airline's weight guidelines, and she also felt much better about her appearance. She maintained her weight, and her binge-purge cycles, for the next few years. It seemed like a constant struggle. To make matters worse, she had broken up with her boyfriend. At this point she felt really depressed, worse than in college. She felt so despondent that she cried virtually every day and occasionally missed work. She frequently had suicidal thoughts, but she never made any actual suicide attempts. The episode lasted a couple months and then seemed to lift by itself. But her weakness and dizziness continued and kept getting worse, and it was at this point that she saw her doctor.

CONCEPTUALIZATION AND TREATMENT

Jill herself recognized the clear indications of bulimia nervosa in her behavior as outlined in the DSM-IV-TR criteria. Her frequent binge eating and purging easily exceeded the minimum average of two binges per week for three months; she compensated for her binge eating by purging, in her case through vomiting and abuse of laxative and diuretics; she experienced fluctuating body weight; and she had an almost constant concern with her body image. Most bulimics are fully aware of the unusual nature of their behavior; many even know the formal diagnostic label of their disorder. Nevertheless they report feeling unable to control their binge-purge cycles. Not all bulimics purge themselves, however. Some compensate for their binge eating by fasting, severe dieting, or excessive exercise.

Jill's history contains many social and occupational pressures that induced her to focus on her weight and appearance, particularly her job as a flight attendant. For the past 10 years bulimic eating has been an effective way for Jill to control her

179

weight, and it seems reasonable to conclude that these factors may have contributed to her development of bulimia nervosa.

After her evaluation interview, Jill was admitted as an outpatient to the eating disorders clinic. The initial focus of therapy was to alter Jill's bulimic eating pattern. Jill's cognitive-behavioral therapy incorporated three general goals: (1) to identify the circumstances that surround her binge eating, (2) to restructure her thoughts about herself and her eating, and (3) to educate her on the risks of bulimic behavior, on meal planning and nutrition, and on an awareness of cultural standards that may contribute to her bulimic behavior.

First, Jill was instructed to keep a detailed food record (which she called her "eating diary") of where, when, and what she ate. This would tell her therapist the exact conditions that were associated with her binge eating. Jill was also instructed to note her moods in this record to see if her emotions were associated with her bulimic behavior. Jill's record showed that she frequently binged in the late afternoon and early evening, often after a particularly long or stressful flight. Her emotional entries in her record also showed that she felt a sense of relief following her binge-purge episodes. By analyzing this record, it was evident that Jill's bulimic behavior was often used as a coping mechanism for stressful life events.

Second, Jill's distorted and illogical self-cognitions regarding her body image and self-worth were addressed using a cognitive restructuring procedure. Through confrontational, Socratic dialogues in individual therapy, Jill was taught to review her thoughts and feelings, to identify her distorted or illogical thoughts, and to adopt more realistic and less self-critical standards. Some of these disordered cognitions emerged in the course of therapy, others were taken from her record.

> **Jill:** Well, here's one from my diary. When I tried on a pair of slacks, they were too tight. I felt really fat, and I was miserable for the rest of the day. I just felt worthless.
> **Therapist:** Did you consider other possibilities?

Jill: Like what?

Therapist: Maybe the slacks shrank in the laundry. Maybe it was humid and sticky, and they just felt tight. Or maybe they were just too small to begin with.

Jill: Sure, I guess it's possible, but I don't know. I mean, they fit before. I thought it meant that I was getting really fat.

Therapist: OK. Let's say that you really did gain a few pounds. So what?

Jill: So what!? It shows that I have to diet even harder because I'm getting obese.

Therapist: Let's look at some of your assumptions. It sounds to me like you have no middle ground; gaining a few pounds means being obese. Do you think that's really an indication of obesity?

Jill: Well, no, I guess not. But you know what I mean.

Therapist: It sounds to me like you have a lot of assumptions about gaining weight. For instance, you feel that gaining a few pounds will make you a failure, and no one will love you or accept you if you do. Is that true?

Jill: Yeah, but some of it's true. The airline might ground me if I get too fat. I mean, it's a real worry.

Therapist: Then maybe being a flight attendant is not the right career for you.

Jill: But I like it. I don't want to quit.

Therapist: I'm not saying you have to. All I'm saying is that you should look at what it's doing to you and maybe consider other possibilities. OK?

Jill: OK.

In addition to her individual therapy, Jill attended group sessions. Mostly these group sessions focused on sharing experiences with other bulimics and fostering a sense of mutual support. In particular, the group members discussed the difficulty they had in controlling their binge eating, and they offered to be available should any member of the group need support or encouragement.

As a further aid to changing Jill's self-critical cognitions, a psychiatrist in the treatment group prescribed the SSRI antidepressant fluoxamine (Prozac). Adjunctive medication is often very helpful in altering distorted, negative thought patterns. It was thought that medication would be especially helpful to Jill, given her vulnerability to developing depressive episodes.

The third goal of therapy was to provide Jill with information regarding various aspects of her eating disorder. First, her therapist described the emotional and physical risks inherent in the binge-purge cycle, such as social isolation, dizziness, electrolyte imbalances, gastrointestinal irritations, and tooth decay. Second, Jill was taught to plan reasonable meals for herself. No wonder she was feeling weak and dizzy! She was given homework assignments that required her to research the nutritional value of various foods and formulate healthy meal plans. Most importantly, she was to actually eat these meals. Third, Jill was taught to recognize our culture's expectations and norms regarding appearances and weight. In Jill's case, the norms of her airline were clear and explicit. For most bulimics, however, the expectations of our society, often conveyed through the entertainment and advertising industries, are more subtle and difficult to identify.

Jill was treated for a total of 10 weeks. For the first two weeks her meals were planned for her. She found it difficult to follow these plans without binge eating now and then; she vomiting eight times after meals during the first two weeks. Still, Jill was making progress over her pretreatment rate. For the next several weeks Jill devised her own meal plans with the help of the staff. She found that having planned her own meals made it a little easier to stick to the diet. Gradually she reduced the frequency of her vomiting until she went through the seventh week without vomiting. After three weeks of relatively normal eating behavior free of purges, Jill discontinued treatment, with follow-up appointments scheduled for 3, 6, and 12 months. She was encouraged to follow her meal plan and to contact her therapist or a therapy group member if she felt that she was having trouble controlling her eating behavior.

PROGNOSIS

Jill's treatment appears to have been effective in altering her bulimic eating patterns. At her 3-month follow-up appointment, Jill stated that she had only binged and vomited twice since ending her treatment. She ate healthier and more balanced meals, both at home and during her layovers, and she felt more energetic and active. Jill also said she felt better about herself and her appearance, and she did not feel as stressed after difficult flights. In short, therapy seems to have greatly reduced the frequency of Jill's binge eating and purging, and it seems to have created enhanced feelings of self-worth that may help prevent these symptoms from reappearing in the future.

At her 12-month follow-up, she reported having had only two or three binges in the past six months, and no purges. She felt better about herself, and she became involved in a steady relationship. She was having some problems staying within the airline's strict weight standards and this caused some distress, but she now wondered if the best choice for her would be to find a different job without such a constant source of stress. At her request her medication was discontinued, and she was instructed to return for treatment if the need arose.

Despite Jill's obvious improvement, however, her prognosis must remain guarded. Bulimia nervosa is a persistent eating disorder, and it has proved to be difficult to effect lasting behavioral changes. Relapse rates during the first year are about 50 to 60 percent. However, although fewer than half refrain from the binge-purge cycle altogether, most report significant improvements in their

183

eating habits, and fully three-fourths no longer meet *DSM-IV-TR* criteria for Bulimia Nervosa. So, even though she may not end her disordered eating entirely, it is likely that her eating will be greatly improved.

ON THIN ICE

I can take all the madness the world has to give,
But I won't last a day without you.

Most of you reading this chapter are probably too young to have heard of Karen Carpenter. This drummer, singer, and songwriter (her lyrics are quoted above) formed a band with brother Richard called simply The Carpenters. It may surprise you to learn that they were the top band in the decade from 1970 to 1980 with 3 Grammy Awards, 5 Platinum Albums, 8 Gold Albums, and 10 Gold Singles. Outwardly she was always joyful and sweet, and she spent her life trying to please others. And it was this need to be accepted—to be perfect—that led to her death.

Karen did not have a naturally thin body shape, and she had always been a little chubby growing up. Apparently she was not happy with her weight, for at age 17 her physician put her on a diet where she lost 20 pounds, from 140 to 120. But it wasn't until after she was famous that she really had problems with her eating and her weight. After reading a review that referred to her as "chubby," she became obsessed with losing weight until by age 25 she weighed a mere 80 pounds and was so weak that she once collapsed on stage. Taking this as a wake-up call, she then sought the help of multiple therapists over the next 7 years and endured many different therapies until her weight had climbed to 108. This was her weight when she died of cardiac failure at the age of 32, the direct result of the strain of 15 years of dieting and starving herself.

Before 1983 Anorexia Nervosa received little attention in the professional literature. But her death focused a clinical and research spotlight on the disorder that increased public awareness and resulted in the establishment of eating disorders clinics across the U.S.

PRESENTING COMPLAINT

Casey collapsed during her regular 5:00 a.m. practice session at the rink. Her father, who had custody that morning, rushed out onto the ice. Her coach was already at her side. When she couldn't be roused, they called 9-1-1, and she was taken to Children's Hospital Denver, not far from her home in Englewood. On the way, the emergency squad gave her saline, suspecting she was dehydrated. She woke up in the Emergency Department, alert but exhausted. The resident on call ordered an electrocardiogram (EKG) and a complete blood count (CBC), but she could find nothing wrong with her heart or her blood gasses. However, she noted that Casey looked emaciated. Indeed, Casey weighed only 91 pounds. This weight was at the seventh percentile for girls her height (5 feet, 5 inches) and yielded a body mass index (BMI) of 15.1, well within the anorexic range, which is any BMI under 17.5. Alarmed, the resident consulted with the supervising attending doctor, and they agreed to have her admitted.

A special 1800-calorie daily diet was prepared for Casey, but she refused to eat most of it, claiming that it tasted bad and that it would "make me fat." By resorting to liquid supplements and IV glucose as well as a stern "come to Jesus" lecture by her attending physician, the staff had added 6 pounds within the week. Although she was still within the anorexic range, she was deemed stable and released to a local residential facility that offered an intensive outpatient program.

PERSONAL HISTORY

Casey is the eldest of two daughters. Her early upbringing was considered unremarkable, with no history of abuse or trauma until the time of her parents' divorce. She and Ellie, her 11-year-old sister, split their time between their mother's apartment and their father's house. Casey was always a well-behaved girl who worked hard to get good grades and stay active in school clubs. She was not particularly popular, but she had a few close friends. She was considered supportive and loyal, but everyone agreed that she also had a strong stubborn streak. Casey would do anything for her family or her friends, but it had to be done her way.

Ever since she was in kindergarten, Casey has loved to skate. She practiced three times a week, usually at the most horrible hours. By the time she was ten, she was competing in regional events. During her parents' divorce, she seemed to find comfort, even escape, in her skating. As her mother struggled with the demands on a single parent and her father paid more and more attention to his new wife and their new baby stepbrother, her rink time became less consistent, though both parents made efforts to keep her involved. They also seemed too busy to really listen to her new coach, who was concerned that she was getting too thin. Lately, he said, her performance began to suffer due to her constant exhaustion and weakness.

She wasn't always so underweight. Casey was at her highest weight as recently as two years ago. She weighed about 130, yielding a BMI of 21.6. One day some hockey players watching her practice called her "Thunder Thighs," and she was horrified. Although her weight was well within the range of 20–22, where most women feel comfortable with their weight, Casey was convinced that she was too fat. She started dieting by severely restricting her food intake, eating virtually nothing but water and vegetables for most meals. She also increased her activity, adding running and swimming to her skating practices. Unbeknownst to her parents, she also vomited and abused laxatives. By her fourteenth birthday her weight was down to 106 (BMI = 17.6, twentysecond percentile). Despite this borderline-anorexic weight, the waif-like skater continued to diet, exercise excessively, and abuse laxatives until she passed out on the ice.

CONCEPTUALIZATION AND TREATMENT

Casey's entrance into the residential facility brought her into contact with a group of professionals who would become central to her life for the next three years. In charge of her team was her psychiatrist, a no-nonsense professional with over 20 years of experience treating patients with eating disorders. Also on the team were a nutritionist, a psychologist, and two team leaders. Therapy included medication, individual counseling, and group sessions.

Medication for anorexic patients is a tricky business. First of all, the medication of choice is food. However, a variety of other medications are often tried. Most common are antidepressants, which have the dual advantage of addressing underlying self-esteem issues as well as having a side effect of weight gain. Because no medications are specifically approved for anorexia, and patients are very hesitant to try medications (for both loss of control as well as the weight gain side effect), extreme care must be taken. Doses start very small (often as little as one-tenth the usual starting dose), and psychiatrists proceed gently, using their intuition as well as their knowledge. Casey's psychiatrist decided to start with liquid paroxetine (Paxil), starting at 1 mg. Once Casey accepted this, the dose was gradually increased to the typical dose of 20 mg. Although the FDA has warned against using Paxil for patients younger than 18, her psychiatrist felt confident in this approach.

The nutritionist focused on psychoeducation, explaining to Casey what healthy weight norms are, how to identify signs of being underweight, creating a balanced diet, and suggesting liquid supplements. Casey's response was typical of most anorexia sufferers: She was interested in the information provided by the nutritionist, understood the possible dangers of malnutrition, and agreed to adhere to a diet that ultimately provided her with 2000 calories daily. And yet, outside the nutritionist's office, she did everything possible to restrict her eating. Often foods were left uneaten, and she occasionally vomited after meals.

The staff clinical psychologist focused mostly on Casey's persistent image of herself as being overweight despite the fact that her BMI placed her in the anorexic range. A related issue was her irrational fear of becoming fat. These distorted negative cognitions are very common among anorexia sufferers, and their very irrationality and persistence make this aspect of therapy frustrating. And yet, Casey's psychologist understood that reacting negatively would be fundamentally counterproductive; a central element in recovery is the development of a trusting, mutually respectful relationship with a professional. This relationship is likely to last for years—long past discharge from the residential center. In many ways, this relationship is the glue that will stay consistent throughout the ups and downs of her therapy.

Casey's team leaders are in charge of the morning and afternoon group sessions. Here the patients share their experiences, both their successes and their setbacks. They also determine weight goals for patients and administer rewards for progress toward their goals. Casey's leaders, Denise and Tonya, determined a goal weight for her of 106 pounds. This would result in a BMI of 17.6, which would officially take her out of the anorexic range. Rewards in the form of privileges (e.g., choosing her favorite craft project to work on) are administered for every half pound gained. And, of course, every half pound is a step closer to her goal weight.

Anorexia is a secretive disorder. Most attempt to hide their disorder in a variety of ways, from wearing loose, baggy clothes to lying about food intake to secretly vomiting after meals. Thus it was surprising to Casey that there were other girls—and one boy—who had pretty much the same issues. The residents all had their own stories, but most seemed more or less like her. Casey was outwardly friendly and outgoing, but she carried around secrets she didn't share with others. The supportive atmosphere of the groups allowed even Casey to open up and discuss her biggest hopes and darkest fears. She talked about the cruel comment from the hockey players that seemed to trigger her need to lose weight. She discussed the sadness and frustration she felt from her parents' divorce, especially feeling unimportant when they got too busy with their new, hectic lives.

After three weeks Casey reached her goal weight of 106, and she was "graduated" to the second stage, which consisted of twice-weekly evening group sessions. Tonya led these, though the patients played a greater role in the session, including taking turns leading the discussion. Now weight was monitored weekly, and rewards came in the form of positive feedback from other group members. In addition, the nutritionist attended the group monthly to provide group psychoeducation and to help monitor patient progress.

Casey continued to gain weight during the second stage of treatment, but at a slower rate. Still, after another four weeks, Casey had gained four pounds and was now at about 110 pounds. At this point she progressed from the second stage of treatment to a weekly support group run by patients. She stayed active in the support group for about 18 months, but gradually she stopped coming.

After her discharge from residential treatment, she continued seeing her clinical psychologist, first weekly and then gradually tapering off to biweekly and then monthly. As always, the primary focus of therapy was increasing her self-esteem and challenging her negative body image. One hope of the psychologist was to encourage Casey to increase her involvement in friends and activities. Once her weight had reached 110, she was allowed to resume her competitive skating. Unfortunately, by that time she felt she had lost her competitive edge, and she really never got back to it.

She also continued seeing her psychiatrist after leaving residential treatment, primarily for monthly medication checks. These appointments gradually became less frequent. After about two years, Casey discontinued her Paxil.

By the beginning of her senior year in high school, Casey still weighed about 110. Her grades were good, but she never again got the straight A's that she did before her hospitalization. In the fall she began dating seriously for the first time. She started staying out late, and sometimes she didn't return home in the mornings. She was also beginning to lose weight again, but slowly, and in the rush of events no one from her family noticed. Outwardly she was happy and appeared in good health, and she was looking forward to starting college at the University of Colorado in Boulder.

When Casey started college, she weighed 103. Other students in her dorm thought she looked thin when school started, and she just seemed to get worse as the semester wore on. Her first problem was with her boyfriend, who had gone to Colorado State. As their relationship dissolved, so did Casey's emotional state, and she started losing weight. She became convinced that he stopped loving her because she weighed too much, and she began starving herself and using laxatives. Shortly after her break-up, she was raped at a fraternity house during a wild party that got out of hand. At first Casey tried to deny any problems, but after missing classes for three days and crying constantly, she made an appointment at the student health service.

Her therapist, a graduate student under supervision by a faculty member, was shocked at her skeletal appearance. Although the primary focus of the evaluation was the rape trauma, the therapist made sure to ask questions related to anorexia. As she suspected, Casey had stopped menstruating a few months ago, and it appeared that her hair was beginning to thin. When asked how she liked herself and her current weight, Casey grew suspicious. The therapist retreated, explaining that rape often affected self-image. The therapist consulted with her supervisor, and she suggested that anorexia was a likely diagnosis and that Casey should be urged to get medical attention. But Casey never came back.

PROGNOSIS

Five days later, Casey's roommate found her lying unconscious on the floor of their dorm room and she ran for the resident assistant. He called 9-1-1, but this time help came too late. She had put too much strain on her heart, and she died of cardiac arrest shortly after being admitted to the hospital.

A QUIET FOG

PRESENTING COMPLAINT

Jake just finished his freshman year at the University of Washington, and he felt like a failure. He had gotten a 2.4 GPA, not terrible, but not close to what was expected of him. He felt discouraged and confused, and he was urged to seek therapy by his parents. Jake obviously didn't want to be seeing a psychologist. It wasn't clear whether he was resistant to therapy or whether he was just embarrassed at having his parents take him to counseling. One thing was certain; he was quiet.

In contrast, his parents released a torrent of words describing the problems with their middle son: he was lazy, unmotivated, stubborn, disorganized. His brothers were successful at school, as his parents had been, but Jake got only slightly above a B-average in high school, and now it was B's and C's. Growing up he seemed smart, but often he sabotaged his grades by forgetting to do his homework, quitting in the middle of assignments, and not finishing tests. Most infuriating, when he did manage to complete a project, often he would leave it behind or lose it. It seemed like he was doing everything he could to get bad grades. His parents also complained about his attitude toward others, noting that he was constantly late for everything and didn't seem to care about making everyone else wait for him. It wasn't that he couldn't pay attention; they noticed that he could be engrossed in TV or a computer game or his running so much that he sometimes didn't notice anything else, but when it came time to do his homework, he didn't have the same kind of focus. They were clearly angry, but they also recognized that his behavior could be due to a psychological problem. Maybe he was oppositional, or passive-aggressive, or anxious, or depressed, or maybe even on drugs. Yet although their words conveyed deep concern, somehow their tone of voice made their questions seem more like accusations than worries.

193

Case 19

When the psychologist spoke with Jake alone, he seemed like the nice, polite kid who entered the office. He agreed that he didn't get the good grades his brothers did. When he was younger he got pretty good grades, and in elementary school he thought of himself as smart. But his grades had been slipping gradually over the years and especially after transitioning from one school level to the next: from elementary school to middle school, middle school to high school, and this year from high school to college. Now he thought of his intelligence as "pretty average, I guess, maybe even on the dumb side." He had a small but supportive group of friends, and he was involved in a wide variety of sports and school activities. He denied any involvement with delinquents or experience with drugs. The whole thing had him confused; he seemed to get stuff in class all right, but he was always forgetting things, or losing things, or his mind was just wandering off to different topics or just daydreaming.

Jake:	Well, it's weird. Sometimes I know I should focus on something, but my mind just wanders off.
Therapist:	Are you ever really focused?
Jake:	Sure. I can play video games for hours, and I don't even notice anything else. TV is the same. I think having that box to look at kind of blocks out everything else.
Therapist:	What do you do when you need to study?
Jake:	At home I used to listen to music, which seemed to block out a lot of distractions around the house. At school I can't study in my room; I have to get a study carrel at the libes.
Therapist:	That blocks out everything else?
Jake:	Not always, but it helps.

PERSONAL HISTORY

Jake lives in an intact family in an affluent suburb of Seattle. His father is a professor of Sociology at the University of Washington; his mother is a CPA who works part time for a local accounting firm. Jake's older brother, Eric, recently graduated from Brown University and has been accepted to Yale Law School. His younger brother, Matt, just finished his sophomore year in high school with straight A's.

According to his parents, Jake had a normal childhood without any significant events or issues, aside from his academic problems. His birth was without any significant incident, and there were no remarkable physical, medical, or behavioral problems they could recall. Socially he seemed to get along with other kids his age, but he was always on the periphery of the social group, never in the center. He kept active playing football and soccer and had become proficient at oboe. There was no indication of any alcohol or drug problem. They concluded that generally he was a good kid, but he just seemed disorganized and sometimes just lazy.

Jake denied any history of abuse or trauma. His parents, especially his father, always expected superior academic performance, and they became increasingly frustrated with him over the years. He felt guilty and depressed because he knew he was letting them down. He would occasionally get frustrated with his brothers, but nothing he considered unusual. When asked about his social interactions with peers, Jake said things were "all right." He got along with others but was never really popular. He had a girlfriend in high school but wasn't dating anyone now. Jake denied any drug problems. He drank at school, but usually just on weekends, and he only got drunk once or twice during his first year. He tried marijuana a few times but didn't really like the feeling. After some gentle prodding, he admitted that on two occasions he tried some medication prescribed for a student down the hall who had been diagnosed with ADHD (Attention-Deficit Hyperactivity Disorder) and that it had been "like night and day." He remembers thinking, "Oh, so *this* is how normal people think."

Case 19

CONCEPTUALIZATION AND TREATMENT

Well, that was enough for Jake's psychologist; a diagnosis of Attention-Deficit Disorder (ADD) was highly likely. Still, he would need to administer a series of screening measures to confirm this diagnosis and to clarify some of the other issues in Jake's life, particularly his low self-esteem.

Several biological and psychological conditions can produce symptoms similar to what Jake is describing, and these should be evaluated. One possibility is a medical problem that interferes with attention, such as hypoglycemia or a medication reaction. Another possibility is that Jake may suffer from a specific learning disability. It may be that Jake's IQ is lower than that of his parents and siblings, which would manifest itself as a relative deficit in his academic performance. Finally, emotional problems such as depression and anxiety can significantly impact attention. This latter factor brings up a chicken-and-egg problem, though. Is Jake's mood depressed because of the years of frustration and failure caused by his ADD, or is his attention disrupted by a chronic depression and low self-esteem? At this point, the two are inextricably mixed.

Because of the complex nature of ADD/ADHD problems, a variety of measures are needed to develop a good picture of the person's condition. A comprehensive evaluation for an attention-deficit problem would take place at a clinic that specializes in that issue and would include first and foremost a detailed clinical interview, preferably with the person and people who are familiar with the person's performance in a variety of settings (e.g., parents, teachers, friends). The evaluation would also include a thorough physical history and exam, intelligence testing, achievement testing, neuropsychological testing, and screening for mental problems.

Therapists in private practice rarely have the time or resources to conduct such a lengthy evaluation, and most are comfortable formulating a diagnosis based on less stringent standards. In Jake's case, his therapist first interviewed Jake and his parents. During the interview with his parents, Jake was filling out a brief questionnaire battery that included tests for anxiety, anger, depression, as well as a checklist specifically developed to assess attention-deficit issues: the Conner's Adult ADHD Rating Scales (Conners, Erhardt, and Sparrow, 1999). This scale has versions for self-ratings as well as ratings by others, so when Jake was being interviewed, his parents each filled out a parent version of the CAARS. The therapist quickly scored these measures, and the results were as he expected: mild anxiety, minimal anger, moderate depressive issues concerning low self-esteem, and significant ADD.

The therapist then outlined a four-pronged treatment plan. First, Jake would benefit from a medication evaluation by either his pediatrician or a psychiatrist on staff at a specialized clinic. There are several choices for medications, including Ritalin, Adderall, and Straterra, all strong stimulants that promote organization and paradoxically decrease hyperactivity. Since Adderall appeared to be helpful before, this would be a logical choice of medication should the physician who evaluates him deem it appropriate. Jake's therapist reiterated that any medication should be taken only under the close supervision of a physician. This is particularly important for attention-deficit medications, that are strong stimulants that have high addiction potentials and the possibility of severe adverse reactions.

The second prong of treatment teaches cognitive and behavioral strategies specific to improving organization and focus. For example, Jake might be instructed to purchase an erasable wallboard where he would write his assignments for the week. Many students carry personal paper or electronic organizers, but a wall-mounted one would be less likely to be overlooked. Other strategies would involve relying more on external structure rather than the person's own sense of organization. For example, work-study jobs that involve individual tasks in a tightly structured schedule would be better than unstructured positions with multiple task demands. So, when Jake applies for work-study jobs next semester, it would be better to work updating catalog entries at the library rather than being a waiter at the student union.

The third prong involves setting up an official individual education plan (IEP) at the university. ADD and ADHD are covered under Section 504 of the Rehabilitation Act of 1973 and also under the Americans with Disabilities Act of 1990. The purpose of these laws is to prevent discrimination against people with attention-deficit problems by having schools (or employers in the case of working adults) set up classroom (or workplace) accommodations that allow these people to function successfully. In Jake's case, his IEP may include provisions such as: having more time to complete exams, taking exams in a private setting free of distractions, having the services of a tutor to instruct him in time management and personal organization skills, and so on.

The fourth element of Jake's treatment plan would be individual psychotherapy to address his self-esteem issues. Jake obviously comes from a family where academic achievement is of utmost importance, and exceptional performance is taken for granted. It is not surprising that his self-worth has been battered over the years. The goal would be to have Jake (and hopefully his family) gradually accept his limitations and learn to see himself as responsible and successful.

After outlining this four-pronged treatment plan, Jake's therapist surprised the family by suggesting that he not see Jake himself. Instead he recommended referring Jake to the student health service at UW. First of all, UW has an excellent clinic with a national reputation, and they could perform a much more thorough evaluation and follow-up than he could. Mostly, though, Jake was already covered for all services under his student health fees. Comprehensive evaluations and psychological treatment can easily cost thousands of dollars. Jake's therapist felt there was no need for the family to incur these costs when they are already covered under his student health insurance plan.

The therapist had Jake fill out a form releasing information to the UW health service so he could fill them in on his evaluation and findings. He also asked Jake to come back after his next semester to update him on his progress.

PROGNOSIS

DSM-IV-TR contains four diagnostic categories for attention-deficit problems: those that are primarily hyperactive/impulsive in nature, those that are primarily inattentive/distractible in their presentation, those that are a mix of these two types, and finally those that cannot be categorized as any of these three subtypes. Jake's therapist diagnosed him with Attention-Deficit Disorder, Inattentive Type. These disorders range in severity from mild to severe. At the one extreme are people who think of themselves as forgetful or disorganized and never seek formal treatment; at the other extreme are children who cannot control their behavior for even brief periods in any social or school setting.

Jake seems to have a moderate form of ADD. It is not surprising that he was not diagnosed until college. First of all, without any overt hyperactivity, there is little reason that his behavior would attract the attention of his teachers or family. As is the case with many ADD sufferers, especially those of higher IQ, Jake's intelligence and hard work enabled him to compensate for his attention difficulties. As students progress through school, they are expected to develop their organizational skills as their assignments and tasks become more complex and loosely structured (e.g., writing term papers on complex social issues rather than answering worksheets on specific topics). Jake was able to compensate for his attention problems to some extent by working harder and longer, but he could not maintain the exceptional grades that was expected in his family and indeed that came easily to him earlier.

With medication and an IEP, there is every reason to expect Jake to be successful. However, ongoing supportive psychotherapy is important for Jake to feel good about himself and his attainments, even if they don't equal the standards set by his high-achievement family.

I CAN'T LIVE WITHOUT YOU

PRESENTING COMPLAINT

Eva is a 10-year-old fifth-grader in a middle-class suburb of Chicago. In February Eva contracted a mild case of pneumonia, which kept her home for two weeks. During this time she had the undivided attention of her mother. On the day before Eva was scheduled to return to school, she complained of severe abdominal pain. This pain was so severe that she could barely walk, let alone go to school. Eva was taken to the emergency room of the local hospital, but the physician on call could find nothing wrong with her. Still, she complained of fever, headaches, and diarrhea. She was allowed to stay home one week longer. Throughout the week Eva's complaints persisted, and her parents took her to her pediatrician three times. However, neither the parents nor the pediatrician could find any objective evidence of any physical illness; her temperature was normal, she did not cough or have any difficulty breathing, she did not go to the bathroom more than usual, and her appetite and sleep seemed good. With the recommendation of Eva's pediatrician, her parents now insisted that she return to school. Eva flatly refused and began throwing tantrums. She carried on for hours, complaining that she still was not feeling well and that she should not be forced to go back to school when she was so sick. She accused her mother of being cruel and wanting to get rid of her.

Eva had always been a somewhat dependent and demanding child, but she had never acted out to any extent before. Although Eva did not carry on in front of her father like she did with her mother, he nevertheless became very concerned about her refusal to go to school. After another week of refusing to go to school—

Case 20

making a total of five weeks of staying home—Eva's parents decided to contact a local psychiatrist who specialized in childhood disorders.

Eva's mother took her to her initial interview at the psychiatrist's office. When the mother came in and sat down next to Eva, she was asked to remain in the waiting room. She left after some hesitation and obvious concern. Eva then described how she felt about the events of the last few weeks. She was unusually articulate and self-disclosing for a girl her age; she began by saying, "OK. Let's start at the beginning."

From Eva's viewpoint her problem was much more involved than just refusing to go to school. At first she complained that she was still sick with a fever of "almost 100" and diarrhea that would strike twice a day. She was very angry with both her mother and her pediatrician for expecting her to go back to school. They did not appreciate how sick she felt and did not take her complaints seriously. "They just don't understand me. Whatever I say is a joke. I mean, what would happen if I got *really* sick?" Her psychiatrist then asked her for more detail, but Eva interrupted him, saying, "I'm not done yet!" She then described a second problem:

My mind thinks ahead. It's like my mind gets ahead of me. Every time something good happens to me, I think ahead to the bad things that may happen afterwards. It's like a state of shock or fright. Sometimes I'm afraid my mom will get killed or the house will burn down or something. This happens at school a lot. I wish I could jump out the window and run home to help. I call it The Fright. When it happens, I mostly want to be at home where someone can take care of me.

Eva was obviously very upset by The Fright, which primarily involved her morbid preoccupations with her own safety and the safety of her family. Eva could not specify any particular cause for her anxiety; she never witnessed a trauma or was told stories of a family catastrophe or anything like that. The only thing she could really say about The Fright is that it gave her a strong desire to be home, a place she described as secure and protecting.

Eva also explained that she feels "sadness and madness" most of the time. She cries frequently, usually for no reason. She also said that The Fright sometimes wakes her up in the middle of the night, and she has trouble getting back to sleep.

Suicidal ideation is fairly rare in children Eva's age, although the numbers have increased in recent years. When Eva's psychiatrist asked her if she had ever thought of killing herself, she said that she would often tell her mother that she was going to commit suicide. Sometimes she would even feign suicide attempts. For example, two days before her interview she emptied a bottle of aspirin and left it where her mother would find it. She then locked herself in the bathroom with the faucet running, having flushed the aspirin down the toilet. She said that her mother was very frightened and pounded on the bathroom door for several minutes before Eva finally opened it. She claimed that she would never actually go through with a suicide attempt; she just wants to make sure that her mother cares about her.

Finally, the psychiatrist asked her if she had any problems getting along with her friends, with the other children at school, or with her family. She denied that anything or anyone bothers her at school; she said that she has several good friends and that her schoolwork is very easy. Thus, her school avoidance appears to be only a by-product of her separation anxiety and not a problem in and of itself. She also denied any serious interpersonal problems. She apparently got along well with her friends at school, and she seemed to have fairly normal relationships with her two sisters. She said she respected and admired her father, and aside from disliking the fact that he wanted her to go back to school, they had a good relationship. She did, however, complain of problems with her mother. Interestingly, these problems stemmed from the fact that she and her mother were too much *alike.*

Therapist: So, Eva, can you tell me about the troubles you have with your mother?

> **Eva:** She's just like me; we're exactly alike. We're both yellers and screamers, and we have screaming matches all the time.
> **Therapist:** Do you like your mom or do you dislike her?
> **Eva:** Oh, I really like her.
> **Therapist:** Eva, let's pretend you were giving your mom a grade on a pretend report card, OK? What grade would you give her?
> **Eva:** B. No, B+.
> **Therapist:** B+, OK. Why B+?
> **Eva:** Well, she helps me most of the time, and she's good to me, so I gave her a good grade.
> **Therapist:** Why not an A?
> **Eva:** Because she yells at me and jumps to too many conclusions.

PERSONAL HISTORY

Eva is part of a Protestant middle-class family. Her father is a middle-level business executive, and he appears to be responsible and concerned about Eva. He spends time with his children on weekends, but because of his busy work schedule, including frequent business trips, his interactions with them during the week are limited. Her mother has never been employed outside the home; as she put it, "My job is to take care of my girls and worry about their welfare." Eva has two sisters, one older and one younger. Their relationships with each other seem to be fairly normal for children their age; they get into occasional arguments and shouting matches, but on the whole they get along well.

Eva's early childhood was unremarkable. Her mother could think of nothing unusual about it, and her medical records show no indication of any serious or unusual injuries or illnesses. Eva's school history was also unremarkable aside from one thing. At age 4 Eva enrolled in nursery school held for half a day, three days a week. Transportation to and from the nursery school was provided by a carpool organized by some of the parents. Eva's mother remembers that Eva was very reluctant to go into other parents' cars in the carpool. In kindergarten the next year, Eva took a bus to school. In contrast to her uncertainty about taking rides in the carpool, she apparently loved the bus rides, and until now she has had no other school-related problems.

Eva's relationships with her peers do contain some early signs of her separation anxiety, however. Since kindergarten, Eva has attended a summer day camp. Although she has always enjoyed these experiences, she has steadfastly refused to attend an overnight summer camp, which her older sister has done for several summers. Similarly, Eva avoids any overnight stays with friends. Once in second grade she was invited to a slumber party by one of her close friends. All of her friends were invited the party, and she "just had to go." But on the afternoon of the slumber party she complained of leg pains so severe that she could not walk. Her mother took her to an orthopedist that afternoon. The orthopedist could find nothing wrong with her legs, but to be cautious he recommended that she not attend the party. This leg pain has reemerged off and on ever since.

The psychiatrist also interviewed Eva's parents to identify any significant aspects of their histories. Her mother reported a particularly noteworthy event that occurred at age 19. She was driving the family ski boat and not paying close attention when she ran into a large yacht. Eva's mother was almost killed in the accident but eventually recovered fully. Eva has felt guilty and responsible for her mother's welfare ever since. She also has been quite worried about her father, who has had a heart condition for many years. "He could go at any time. I'm constantly waiting for the phone call."

Although Eva's father was concerned for his daughter's welfare, he was personally resistant to the idea of therapy for her, and psychotherapy in general. He met with the psychiatrist only once and was very reluctant to disclose personal information. Eva's mother confided that there is a long history of depression in his family. When asked about this, he flatly denied any history of mental illness in any relative. He made it clear that although he would go along with Eva's treatment, he wanted no part in it personally.

CONCEPTUALIZATION AND TREATMENT

DSM-IV-TR defines separation anxiety disorder as a child's excessive and unwarranted fear about being apart from one or more important attachment figures, usually the mother. This anxiety must have existed for at least four weeks. This disorder can be manifested through a number of symptoms, including unrealistic worries about the welfare of the attachment figures or oneself, complaints of medical symptoms, persistent refusals to be separated from the attachment figures, and a need to be in constant contact with the attachment figures. Eva clearly fit these criteria. As is the case with most children her age, Eva's separation anxiety disorder was manifested primarily in her refusal to go to school.

Other children with separation anxiety exhibit symptoms that were not manifested by Eva. Some have great difficulty in falling asleep without the major attachment figures or complain of frequent nightmares involving their morbid ideation. They might demand to sleep in their parents' bed, or if this is not allowed, they might sleep outside their parents' door. Some cannot stand to be separated from their attachment figures for even small periods of time. They either cling to them most of the day or constantly follow them, a behavior pattern known as "shadowing."

In addition to her separation anxiety, Eva also showed symptoms of a major depressive episode. She complained of depressed mood and a lack of interest in her usual activities. She also complained of feelings of sadness and frustration, frequent crying, early morning awakening, various somatic complaints, and vague suicidal ideation. It is not uncommon for separation anxiety disorder to co-occur with a major depressive episode. The extent of her mood disturbance and her apparent family history of affective disorders suggested the possibility that Eva may be genetically predisposed to depression.

Eva was seen for therapy once a week at the psychiatrist's office. Her therapist formulated a relatively straightforward conceptualization of her case. Her symptoms resulted from her excessive and unwarranted fear that she would be abandoned and left alone. She feared that some catastrophic event would befall her parents, which would leave them unable to care for her. As Eva matured she was confronted with an increasing number of subtle social pressures that she increase her independence, such as attending slumber parties and summer camp. It was apparent that she was unable to cope with these demands.

The primary aim of Eva's treatment was to reduce the neurotic defenses that have thus far inhibited her psychosocial development. The first stage of therapy consisted of three broad, progressive steps. First, Eva's pervasive anxieties, depressed mood, and suicidal ideation were brought under control, in part through medication. Second, her relationship with her mother was stabilized. Third, the psychiatrist worked with Eva's mother to get her to return to school.

The second stage focused on individual psychotherapy, which explored her thoughts and feelings. As these were uncovered and discussed, the therapist provided her with clarifications, reinterpreta-tions, and occasional confrontations. Throughout treatment the psychiatrist provided Eva with emotional support, primarily by reassuring her that she was loved by her parents and that their frustrations and expectations were intended to be for her own good.

The first concrete action taken by Eva's psychiatrist was to put her on a small dose of the SSRI antidepressant citalopram (Celexa). After a week her dose was doubled to the starting adult dose, and later it was raised again to a daily dose of 30 milligrams. After two and a half weeks on Celexa, Eva's suicidal ideation abated, and after another two weeks, her anxiety lessened and her depressive symptoms began to remit. Eva was maintained on Celexa throughout therapy.

The next step was to get Eva back to school. After three further weeks at home, when her medication seemed to be working effectively, it was time to return to school. With both Eva and her mother in session, the psychiatrist made it clear that he expected her to return by the next week. For the first week Eva was allowed to call home for reassurance three times a day; for the next week calls were limited to once a day. With the mother's permission, the school nurse was contacted, and Eva's hypochondriacal symptoms were explained. During the first week Eva called from the nurse's office on three separate days, and her mother picked her up once. But after that first week, she became more comfortable at school and had no further problems. Despite her 8-week absence, she had little trouble catching up on her missed schoolwork. With Eva's return to school, therapy now focused on underlying issues that prompted her anxieties.

Another aspect of Eva's therapy involved several sessions with her mother. Typically both parents are seen, but sometimes one parent, usually the father, may refuse to participate. One goal of the sessions with Eva's mother was to inform her of how her parenting style may have unwittingly exacerbated Eva's symptoms. In particular, she was told to avoid screaming matches with Eva. "How?" she asked incredulously. "It takes two to argue. Just walk away," was the therapist's response. Gradually Eva's relationship with her mother improved; they argued less and Eva became much more obedient.

It was emphasized that Eva's morbid preoccupations were not simply attempts to manipulate her parents; Eva actually feared for her own safety and for the safety of her family. These fears might not have a logical basis, but they were real to Eva. Similarly, Eva's frequent somatic complaints were seen not simply as childish attempts at avoiding things, although of course they often did produce this effect; Eva really did feel pain.

First, Eva's fears were addressed. She was reassured that neither she nor her parents were in any actual serious danger, and that they would be available when she needed them. Eva's perceptions of her parents' demands on her, such as their insisting that she go to school and their suggesting that she attend summer camp, were also discussed. She was told to think of these expectations not as their wish to get rid of her but rather as signs that they really did care for her. They wanted to give her opportunities. They expected her to be a big girl who could take care of herself, and they wanted her to grow up and be successful. By and large Eva reacted favorably when her parents' behavior was explained in this light.

Second, the therapist attempted to uncover Eva's latent feelings. Like most children, Eva found it difficult to express these ideas directly, especially those that involved hostility or anxiety. But she was able to acknowledge her feelings through expressive play. For example, Eva occasionally played with a dollhouse during the therapy sessions. During one session she placed a small doll next to a larger one and labeled the small one Baby and the larger one Mommy. The therapist asked her what the baby was thinking. Eva replied, "The baby is very sad. She thinks that her mother is dying and that she'll be all alone." Eva's underlying cognitions were also expressed through art. During a later session Eva drew a picture of a starfish. "Sea star," corrected Eva. This creature had a broken arm that appeared to be dangling from its body. In the course of describing this picture to the therapist, Eva commented that her family was like the sea star and that she was the broken appendage that was not really a part of the whole. By paying close attention to this sort of simple play example, the therapist was able to assess many of her unconscious fears and motives. As therapy progressed, the therapist was able to uncover and reinterpret many of Eva's core issues, primarily her strong fears of abandonment.

An important aspect of conducting psychotherapy with children is to relate to them from their own frame of reference. Therapists attempt to match their techniques to the cognitive level of the children they treat and to discuss issues that are important to these children. For example, when Eva's psychiatrist discussed the process of growing up, he made sure to put this concept in terms that she would be able to understand. Whereas for older patients growing up may mean learning to handle interpersonal relationships, choosing a career, or making life goals, for Eva growing up meant having a locker of her own and going to different rooms for different school subjects instead of staying with the same teacher all day.

After about six months, Eva's father suggested that her antidepressant medication be discontinued. Her depressive symptoms had long since remitted, and she appeared to be making slow but steady progress in overcoming her anxiety. The psychiatrist responded that, as a general rule of thumb, antidepressant medications are to be continued for at least six months after symptoms have remitted in order to minimize the chance of relapse. They agreed to withdraw her from Celexa in three months. But within two weeks of discontinuing her medication, her depressive symptoms began to reappear. She was then put back on a maintenance dose of 20 milligrams, which she continued to take for over a year.

Over the eight-month course of therapy, Eva's fears of separation gradually diminished. Her morbid preoccupations were rare, and her anxieties no longer interfered with her behavior. At this point Eva discontinued therapy. She still exhibited some mild residual signs of her disorder, such as a refusal to sleep over at friends' houses and a resistance to attending a full-time summer camp. However, most of her more incapacitating anxieties had long since remitted.

PROGNOSIS

Eva made good progress; nevertheless, there are reasons to classify her prognosis as guarded. First, she has an apparent family history of depression and had experienced a rather severe major depressive episode by age 10. Although she responded well to Celexa, a brief interruption in her medication resulted in a rapid reemergence of her symptoms. Taken together, this information indicates that Eva might have a genetic predisposition that will make her vulnerable to depression throughout her life.

Along with this genetic vulnerability comes an environmental factor. Eva's mother is anxious, moody, and somewhat dependent herself. These characteristics may be exacerbated by an aloof, defensive husband, but it is difficult to tell with so little direct contact with him. So although some behavioral changes in her parenting have had a positive impact on Eva's behavior, overall her mother's personality may contribute to Eva's generally negative outlook on life.

A final cause for concern is that Eva's symptoms have not remitted completely; she continues to show subtle signs that her disorder is persisting. In particular she continues to be apprehensive about being away from home for more than a few hours at a time; overnight outings are still out of the question. A history of separation anxiety disorder is a risk factor for developing multiple anxiety disorders in adulthood. It remains to be seen whether these symptoms will fade gradually or whether they will develop into a lifelong pattern of dependency.

The course of this disorder varies widely. Whereas some children will never show any evidence of a separation anxiety after their symptoms recede, others will show subtle residual signs for many years. Many seem to recover completely and function perfectly well throughout high school, but then they begin to show symptoms when they are about to separate from their parents (e.g., when they accept a job or go off to college). Other children manage to separate, but they still feel a strong need to keep in contact. These children will either come home almost every weekend or call their parents frequently, some up to several times every day. In some cases the disorder takes a chronic course. These children never move far away from the family home, and a few never leave the home at all. In these cases, there is almost always an issue of unresolved dependency and overprotection in the parents, who promote their children's behaviors. For these chronic cases, continual contact with their parents, either by living with them, visiting them frequently, or calling them several times a day, becomes a lifelong pattern.

LIFE AFTER MAINSTREAMING

When most people think of mental retardation, they think of school children who face the struggles and opportunities of being mainstreamed into public school systems. This is certainly an important and visible group worthy of public attention, but this age group includes only a minority of those with mental retardation. The vast majority have passed through the public school system. What happens to them now? The following case is one example.

PRESENTING COMPLAINT

Steve has dark, rather lifeless eyes. His thinning gray hair is combed straight back. His yellowed teeth have a pronounced overbite. He has a medium build and is perhaps 40 pounds overweight. His posture is stooped, and he walks with an unsteady, shuffling gait. All in all, Steve, 52, gives the impression of a man in his early 60s in declining health.

Interactions with Steve are difficult. Sometimes he mutters unintelligibly; at other times he begins conversations (to use the term loosely) with loud, startling, and often illogical comments. For instance, recently Steve approached a stranger with a peculiar combination of a welcoming smile and a sideways glance. Suddenly he blurted out, "Are you the dentist?" When the surprised visitor replied that he was not, Steve followed up by shouting even more loudly, "Are you the doctor?" When the answer was again no, Steve became frustrated and impatient. His smile had disappeared, and the sideways glance now held suspicion. "Well, what are you then?" The stranger then explained that he was a student on a visit, adding, "I'm applying for a summer . . ." but Steve interrupted. "A student, that's nice." His eyebrows lifted, and he developed a wide grin. Still grinning, he turned and wandered down the hall to his room.

For the past seven years, Steve has lived in an intermediate care facility (ICF) run by a private agency in New York City. The ICF is a residential group home with seven bedrooms and 12 residents. Steve came to the ICF from a succession of other group residences, including family home care, city-run developmental centers, and a large state-run institution. Steve's behavior in these various facilities has generally been described as uncooperative, stubborn, and aggressive.

Steve's adjustment to the ICF was slow and difficult, and he continued to show his characteristic verbal and physical aggression and a general attitude his counselors described as "finicky." After a year at the ICF, however, Steve had become an integral part of the family and showed a dramatic reduction in his aggression. Although Steve generally stays to himself, there are people at the ICF he would consider his friends, that is, people with whom he interacts regularly and whom he misses when they are absent.

In his seven years at the ICF, Steve has shown a gradual deterioration in his physical health and mental functioning. Physically, his posture has become more stooped, and his gait has become unsteady. Intellectually, Steve has become forgetful and disoriented, and he tends to speak about past events as if they were happening in the present. He has become more suspicious, even paranoid. With increasing frequency he has conversations and even arguments with inanimate objects and imaginary friends.

PERSONAL HISTORY

Steve's parents moved to New York from Puerto Rico two years before he was born; they returned to their native island about 25 years ago. About five years ago Steve's father died. He has very limited contact with his mother, who calls him about once every other month and sends him a card when he is sick. As limited as this contact is, it is rarely initiated by his mother; on most occasions some prodding by the ICF is needed for any contact to be made. Steve has no family in New York aside from a paternal aunt. She used to come for occasional short visits when Steve first arrived at the ICF, but she showed little interest in him or the facility and gradually saw him less and less. Steve has had no visits from any other family member or any friends. As a consequence of this limited social contact, little is known of Steve's early childhood aside from what can be pieced together from school reports and facility records.

Steve did very poorly when he was first enrolled in the New York public school system. He had numerous behavioral problems throughout kindergarten and first grade, including arguments with teachers and fights with fellow students. A history of fire-starting is also noted. His first grade teacher recommended that he repeat first grade, but apparently the principal intervened, and Steve was tested by a child psychiatrist who concluded that Steve was "mentally retarded but trainable," which is roughly equivalent to the DSM-IV-TR diagnosis of Moderately Mentally Retarded. In light of Steve's disruptive behavior, it was recommended that he be placed in a special group home. Apparently his parents agreed, because the records state that he was committed to a city-run developmental center (a small, institution-like residence with 30 beds) at the age of 7.

The staff notes for the developmental center (DC) contain entries that Steve was difficult to control and disruptive to other residents. At age 11 he was transferred to a state-run institution upstate, where he remained until he was 40. As part of a state-mandated program to transfer the mentally ill from institutions to community residences (known as the Willowbrook Consent Decree), Steve was placed in a city-run DC. Compared to the state-run institution, the center offered much more contact with the staff. It also offered a relatively structured program of training in social, academic, and vocational skills, including a supervised workshop. Steve did well in his work setting, where he sorted parts for toys. However, his social skills began to deteriorate, and he was transferred to a smaller residential home setting managed by a couple specially trained in dealing with developmentally disabled residents. In many ways, this home was similar to foster care. Here he was under less behavioral supervision but had more interpersonal contact. Steve continued to work at the workshop while he lived in the residential home. Unfortunately, his social skills continued to decline, and one day he became angry at a counselor at the workshop and struck him, breaking his jaw. Steve was immediately removed from the workshop and his residential home and placed back in the city-run DC, where there is more supervision. After two years he was placed in his present ICF, again as a result of the Willowbrook Consent Decree.

CONCEPTUALIZATION AND TREATMENT

The cause of Steve's mental retardation is unknown. According to current DSM-IV-TR terminology, he would be diagnosed as Moderately Mentally Retarded. His diagnosis has changed little in the past 40 years, other than occasional updates in terminology to remain consistent with current diagnostic manuals. DSM-IV-TR describes mental retardation in terms of four levels of severity: mild, moderate, severe, and profound, based on IQ and to a lesser extent functional limitations. Moderate mental retardation describes people with an IQ in the approximate range of 35–55. As a general rule, this group is unlikely to progress in academic subjects beyond the second-grade level, though with proper supervision they may be able to hold unskilled or semi-skilled jobs. They may be able to perform some basic health care functions (maintaining personal hygiene, doing laundry, etc.), but generally they cannot live independently. They require close supervision when upset or under stress. They seem to adjust best in community-based group homes under moderate supervision.

Treatment for Steve involves pharmacotherapy and behavior modification. Drugs are prescribed mostly in an attempt to manage his aggressive impulses. Over the years he has been prescribed several different medications; currently he is taking paroxetine (Paxil) along with olanzapine (Zyprexa) to reduce his impulsive behavior, particularly his aggressive outbursts. On this combination his outbursts are relatively well controlled without causing undue sedation. However, he has gained about 25 pounds, and that is a concern for his psychiatrist.

Steve's behavior therapy is divided into three aspects. The most formal of these is a token management program of in-house active treatment goals. These goals are themselves divided into three specific categories: self-care, independent living, and academics. The treatment director oversees each resident's individual treatment program.

She begins with a functional assessment covering the following areas: medications, physical functioning (mobility, hearing, etc.), financial status, legal status, developmental history, emotional development, social development, and independent living skills. Based on this assessment, she determines active treatment goals most appropriate for each resident. Self-care goals, for example, range from grocery shopping and doing the laundry for higher functioning individuals down to making the bed or using utensils for lower functioning residents. These goals are posted in the lounge to serve as a reminder for the residents and staff. They are reviewed at least monthly and revised as needed.

One of Steve's current self-care goals is brushing and flossing his teeth. Although he has known how to brush and floss his teeth since childhood, he often does an incomplete job and sometimes forgets altogether. Every time Steve successfully completes his brushing and flossing, he is rewarded with a coin-like token, which he can trade in for after-dinner snacks or special privileges during weekend activities. Steve's primary goal for independent living is to increase his interpersonal skills. He is rewarded for engaging in conversation with other residents, showing concern for others' welfare, and, most of all, controlling his temper. Steve has made the greatest improvements in this area. On the other hand, he has done the worst in his academics. One current academic goal is to count change from purchases, but here he has made little progress. As is the case for many older residents, Steve's intellectual functioning continues to decline with his diminishing health. Often the treatment goal for these patients is the maintenance of existing skills rather than the acquisition of new ones.

In addition to his in-house token management training, Steve participates in adult day programming for six hours a day, five days a week. Every weekday morning Steve joins other residents (who come from other homes as well as Steve's own ICF) in a modified van that serves as a small bus. For two or three hours each day, the group works at a sheltered workshop, where they sort and package combs, brushes, and hair clips. The rest of the time is spent on different group events: picnics, movies, museums, and the like. But not everyone from the IFC goes to this particular day programming. Because of limited space and resources, and because the residents are at somewhat different developmental levels, Steve's ICF must participate in several programs to fulfill the needs of its residents.

Ironically, it may be that the most informal aspect of Steve's therapy may have the greatest impact on his behavior: the social milieu established at the ICF. Located in a residential section of Queens, the ICF is a renovated duplex on a quiet, middle-class street of single-family and two-family homes. The ICF is clean and well maintained; the walls are painted in bright, cheerful colors, and the furniture is new but still has a homey feel. In addition to the seven bedrooms, which the residents decorate themselves, there are three lounges and a group kitchen. The atmosphere is open, friendly, and supportive; staff and residents are addressed by their first names. In many ways, the ICF functions as a large family. Perhaps the least involved member of this family is Steve, but even he has become cooperative and involved over the past several years. The matriarch of this family is the cook, an older neighborhood woman who has been at the ICF since it opened. In addition to preparing the meals, she takes it upon herself to look out for the residents and their home by giving advice, greeting visitors, and performing other helpful tasks. A housekeeper has also been with the ICF for years, but she is less involved with the residents.

Although the atmosphere of the ICF is friendly and informal, the work is very demanding. The direct-care staff consists of a residential manager, a treatment director, and five to six full-time staff members. Burnout is a common problem. And since the ICF can offer only relatively low salaries for its staff, turnover is high; the average staff member stays for only a year or so. Despite this rapid turnover (or perhaps because of it), the staff members are generally responsive and enthusiastic.

PROGNOSIS

The prognosis for Steve is poor, both medically and psychologically. In the past year Steve has shown significant declines in his physical health and intellectual functioning. The treatment director describes him as "getting several years older each year." These declines will of course continue and probably accelerate. His case is complicated by the fact that he has gained so much weight, which contributes to a host of medical problems. Steve is not alone; in general mentally retarded adults are at a higher risk than the general population for a number of negative health consequences. Despite this, mentally retarded adults are living longer than ever, and their numbers in the population have dramatically increased in recent years. This brings up a sociological problem: their parents are growing correspondingly older. Parents who care for their mentally retarded children naturally find it more and more difficult to manage as they age. Worst of all, over half of these parents make no plans for their children's care after their own deaths. These parents, like Steve's, will simply leave matters to the state to decide.

It can be argued that Steve's treatment over the past 45 years has been affected more by legal regulations than by medical and psychiatric advances. Judicial and legislative mandates that set specific standards for the treatment of this population were prompted by three factors: the growing numbers of mentally retarded adults, their special psychiatric and medical needs, and the uncovering of past institutional abuses. Without doubt this policy of active government intervention has raised the general standard of treatment for the mentally disabled and has enabled thousands of

219

mentally retarded adults to move from large institutions to relatively small community residences. It is precisely because of such a government mandate that Steve enjoys the relative freedom and autonomy of his IFC.

IN A WORLD OF HIS OWN

PRESENTING COMPLAINT

Tommy is a cute 5-year-old boy with straight brown hair and bright blue eyes. Except for his slightly crooked teeth, he looks just like any other boy his age. But after one watches Tommy for just a short time, it becomes apparent that he is not a normal boy. His blank expression is the first clue of the severe abnormalities that affect almost every aspect of his life: his speech, his thinking, his actions, and his relationships with others.

The most obvious sign of Tommy's psychological impairment is his speech. Except for occasional incoherent groans, Tommy is mute. In the first five years of his life he has learned only a few signed words using American Sign Language (ASL). He can gesture for "more," "eat," and "toilet," the latter by signing the letter "T." He also tries to communicate by pointing at people, places, and objects, but most often the intent of these nonspecific gestures is unclear. Other than these rudimentary sounds and gestures, Tommy has no real linguistic ability.

Tommy's IQ is 48, as measured on the Wechsler Preschool and Primary Scale of Intelligence (WPPSI-III) (Wechsler, 1991). This score would categorize him as moderately retarded. Realistically, though, this score is only a rough estimate. Because of his pervasive lack of communication skills and his lack of interest in testing procedures, it is difficult to assess the actual extent of his cognitive impairment with any accuracy.

What is easier to assess is Tommy's odd behavior. For one thing, there's his repetitive behavior. Frequently Tommy will sit with his arms grasping his chest or knees and slowly rock back and forth, all the while staring straight ahead. Tommy also engages in other forms of repetitive behavior such as pushing a toy car back and forth (often not on its wheels) and drawing page after page of parallel straight lines. It is not uncommon for these seemingly meaningless behaviors to last for two or three hours without interruption. At these times Tommy shows little emotion and seems totally engrossed in his ritualistic behavior. In the past few months, Tommy's hand has become the central focus for many of his strange behaviors. He will suddenly stop what he is doing, hold his hand directly in front of his face, and intensely stare at it while rotating it slowly. As he examines his hand, he sometimes emits a high-pitched squealing tone; occasionally he smiles and giggles. Usually, though, he simply stares at it. He seems to be especially interested if his hand is wet and dripping or covered with food, which is often the case at mealtimes.

In addition to these strange, repetitive behaviors, Tommy also has bursts of wild, uncontrolled activity, usually when he is upset. Sometimes he will run around the perimeter of the room with his legs pumping and his arms flailing, screaming incessantly. At other times he pounds his hands against the floor or wall in an angry, frustrated tantrum. Often when he is examining his hand he will shake it so violently that it appears that he is trying to separate it from his arm. (This sort of flailing is termed "hand flapping.") On rare occasions Tommy manages to bite his hand while flapping, usually hard enough to break the skin. In the midst of these wild behaviors, Tommy appears to be genuinely upset; his face takes on a grimace and grows red, and his whole body seems tense. When he is restrained during these uncontrolled actions, he usually struggles for a few moments and then inexplicably goes about his business as if nothing ever happened, seemingly oblivious of the person who restrained him.

By far the most tragic aspect of Tommy's disorder, especially to his family, is his complete inability to form interpersonal relationships. During his short life Tommy has never engaged in any meaningful interpersonal communication, not even at the level of establishing sustained eye contact. He seems to understand that people exist, and he even reacts to them occasionally; however, he does not seem to attach any special significance to other people as fellow human beings. For the most part he treats other people like inanimate objects to be noticed, ignored, or avoided, much like most people treat shrubs or pieces of furniture. Tommy appears to attach some special significance to his parents—he will look at them when they address him and will pay attention to their actions. Even this relationship is very distant, though. Perhaps the best description for his relationship with his parents is that he treats them like strangers on a busy city street; he seems to understand that they are fellow humans and may even be temporarily interested in what they are doing, but he seems to have no particular interest in establishing any sort of meaningful relationship with them.

Tommy's parents attempted to care for him at home, but his disruptive behavior became increasingly more unmanageable. At this point he was evaluated at a special school for autistic and emotionally disturbed children.

PERSONAL HISTORY

Tommy is the younger child of two in an upper-middle-class family living in an affluent suburb of Milwaukee. Tommy's father is a senior vice president of a medium-size manufacturing firm, and his mother is an associate professor at a large university. Tommy's brother, who is four years older, is successful in school and popular with his friends.

During his infancy, Tommy's mother described him as a "model baby" who was always quiet and hardly ever cried or fussed. Throughout the first two years of his life, Tommy was usually quiet and independent. However, from early on it was difficult for his parents to get his attention or make eye contact. He was unresponsive to games such as peek-a-boo, and he did not demonstrate any need to be held or comforted. In fact, he completely ignored his parents, his brother, and anyone else who came to visit. Although his parents thought these traits were somewhat peculiar, they did not worry about them at first.

When he was about six months old Tommy was enrolled in day-care. At first he was considered a quiet, cooperative child, but before long his utter failure to interact socially became obvious. He spent the majority of his day silently staring off into the distance. He began to show odd repetitive behavior and to throw angry tantrums. These odd behaviors seriously disrupted the day care routine, and Tommy was required to leave. The day-care staff suggested that Tommy should see a specialist, but Tommy's parents were convinced that his odd behavior was something that he would eventually outgrow. They hired a private sitter to stay with him during the day, but after going through three sitters in only eight months, they knew something had to be done.

By this time Tommy's parents began to worry seriously about his intellectual abilities. He was taken to numerous pediatric and neurology specialists, whose diagnoses were all the same: Tommy suffered from childhood autism. Tommy's parents realized that he needed special care, so they hired a private pediatric nurse to stay with him. Over the next year, Tommy's disruptive behavior became more frequent and more severe. In addition, he began to flap and bite his hand. His parents and the nurse had to monitor his behavior constantly to make sure he did not injure himself. After about a year the private nurse quit, and Tommy's mother was forced to take a semester off work to look after him herself. Finally she contacted a school for autistic and emotionally disturbed children. After being on the waiting list for approximately four months, Tommy was enrolled when a space became available.

CONCEPTUALIZATION AND TREATMENT

The staff at the special school had no difficulty diagnosing him as having autistic disorder. Autistic disorder, commonly referred to simply as "autism," is a pervasive developmental disorder that affects almost every aspect of a child's life. The primary feature of autism, which literally means "self-ism," is the child's inability to form meaningful interpersonal relationships and a more or less complete withdrawal into a private world. This profound social withdrawal is usually accompanied by severe disturbances in the child's intellectual and linguistic abilities; most autistic children are mentally retarded and have very limited communication skills. In addition, autistic children are characterized by odd behaviors, typically consisting of meaningless repetitious behaviors and bursts of wild activity. Many autistic children also engage in self-mutilating behaviors, including hand biting, scratching and gouging, head banging, and pica—eating nonnutritive substances such as paste or feces.

Tommy was enrolled in the school for autistic and emotionally disturbed children in November. During the academic year, the school runs from 8:30 to 4:30 on weekdays. The staff consists of professionals with doctorates or master's degrees in clinical psychology and special education. There are five full-time therapists, three part-time therapists (one occupational therapist and two speech therapists), and several volunteers from local colleges and high schools. The pupils range from 5 to 25 years of age and are drawn from the entire Milwaukee metropolitan area. The number of pupils varies; presently the school is full with 18. Fourteen of the children are autistic. The other four are diagnosed as having Asperger's disorder. Like autistic children, Asperger children exhibit extreme shyness, withdrawal, and anxiety, which seriously impairs their social development. These children are so intimidated by interpersonal situations that their scholastic performance may suffer as well. They also engage in stereotyped or restricted activities, though these are usually not as florid as in autistic disorder. However, emotionally disturbed children differ from autistic children in that they generally have normal cognitive and verbal development.

During the summer Tommy's school runs an eight-week live-in summer camp where the students are supervised for 24 hours a day. The staff at the camp consists of one staff member from the school who acts as a supervisor and six trained undergraduate counselors. The number of students who may attend camp at any one time is limited to seven. Because there is a long waiting list for this camp, the younger and more disturbed children are limited to two weeks at the camp. The older and more capable students are allowed to stay the entire eight weeks. Being the youngest and most severely disturbed child in the school, Tommy was limited to two weeks during his first two summers.

Tommy's school employs a model of treatment based on behavior modification. The primary focus of the staff is not to cure the students but rather to teach them some basic skills that may help them to learn some functional skills. The therapists attempt to achieve this goal by carefully controlling the children's environment, particularly the level of reinforcement and punishment the children receive. The more formal classroom therapy, conducted both in group and individual instruction, concentrates on providing the children with opportunities to develop social and cognitive skills. Lessons in social interaction and basic hygiene are taught through less formal instruction, which is conducted just about anywhere: on the playground, in the cafeteria, and even in the bathrooms. Because therapy relies to such a great extent on controlling the children's social environments, parents are encouraged to adopt behavioral techniques at home to help maintain the changes made at school

Group lessons take several forms; their general aim is to teach these self-absorbed students to cooperate with each other. For example, in a shared finger painting task, each child starts a picture and then exchanges pictures with another student. The children are reinforced for allowing another student to work on "their" project, and they are given special rewards for working on a project together. In another group activity, this time conducted on the playground, students are assigned to either ride on a swing or to push another student. Again, the children are reinforced for displaying coopera- tion and reciprocity. During these sessions the therapists have to be careful to notice whenever a student behaves appropriately and to reinforce that student as soon as possible through encouragement, hugs, and occasional snacks. Just as important, inappropriate or injurious behavior must be stopped immediately.

Individual therapy focuses on developing the children's cognitive and linguistic skills. For example, the therapist might employ flash cards and practice booklets to work on a student's vocabulary or basic math skills. In addition, each child meets with a speech therapist for 50 minutes every other day to practice his or her diction or, in the case of more severely disturbed children, signing. Every student is also instructed in basic vocational skills (e.g., matching wires by colors, sorting various nuts and bolts, sweeping the work area). Getting a job in a sheltered workshop is probably the only employment opportunity most of these children will ever have.

In addition to these relatively formal lessons, the staff takes every opportunity to teach the students basic life skills. During lunch the staff attempts to monitor closely the students' behavior, and students are reinforced for such things as waiting in line cooperatively, eating with others, not playing with their food, chewing their food sufficiently before swallowing, and not causing disturbances (e.g., throwing their food, taking other students' food, running or screaming). Similar practical training takes place in the bathrooms. Although being toilet trained is a requirement for admission to the school, accidents are not uncommon among the younger and more disturbed children. The students have to be carefully monitored to ensure that they perform the common steps of toileting that most people take for granted (putting the toilet seat up or down, making sure to urinate or defecate *in* the toilet and not on or around it, wiping themselves adequately, flushing the toilet, washing afterwards). The staff regards teaching the students these basic life skills as a vital step in developing a greater degree of independence. After all, how long is a sheltered workshop going to keep an employee who constantly soils himself or messes up the bathroom?

Teaching basic life skills is the primary focus of the summer camp. Students, called campers, are taught to perform a variety of everyday tasks that include cleaning their room, doing their laundry, taking a shower, and preparing for bed. Each of these basic tasks is broken up into smaller, more manageable subtasks. For example, getting the campers ready for bed involves several individual components: picking up their toys and clothes, changing into their pajamas, brushing their teeth, and so forth. The other focus of the summer camp is to develop the campers' social skills by providing opportunities for interaction and reinforcing cooperative behavior. This training occurs primarily during recreational activities and at mealtimes.

The school uses a variety of reinforcements to reward appropriate behavior. First and foremost, secondary reinforcement in the form of attention, praise, encouragement, and hugs is given to every student whenever appropriate. However, because one of the primary characteristics of autistic children is a marked disinterest in interpersonal relationships, this social reinforcement is usually supplemented by more tangible rewards such as candy and snacks. As the students become accustomed to the structure of the program, their privileges (recess time, dessert at lunch) become used as reinforcements with increasing frequency. This is especially true at the summer camp, where the students' recreational activities (swimming, hiking, playing games), their participation on field trips, and even their choice of food are contingent on their behavior.

Eliminating inappropriate behavior is more difficult. Because the staff's attention and concern may serve as secondary reinforcers for inappropriate actions, these behaviors are ignored whenever possible. In this way the staff attempts to extinguish the inappropriate behaviors. Negative behavior can be very disrupting to the other students, especially during group lessons, so often this extinction process is carried out by placing the child in a separate room, which is commonly referred to as a time-out room. Occasionally the children are punished by scolding them or withdrawing their privileges. On some occasions they must be physically restrained by the staff to prevent injury or damage. Such an occasion arose when Tommy suddenly ran off the playground and began beating on the back of an elderly man who was walking down the sidewalk.

Occasionally a child exhibits odd behavior that demands close supervision. For example, one autistic girl had a persistent habit involving pica. She would hide in a bathroom stall until no one was around. Then she would defecate, reach down and grab her own feces, and quickly begin eating. The staff learned to keep a close eye on her. When they noticed that she was not with the other students, they would immediately run to the nearest bathroom and would often catch her in the act. Her habit took on the air of an addiction; when she ate her own excrement, she smiled, giggled, and became very upset when she was interrupted. The staff was careful to prevent this behavior and reinforce her for flushing her feces. Over the course of four months, her pica was eliminated.

Tommy was extremely upset when he first came to the school. He threw frequent tantrums, about four or five per day, and spent most of his time flapping his hand or rocking quietly in a corner. Soon he became accustomed to the school routine, though, and it became possible to engage him in the daily lessons. By the holiday break in December, Tommy had grown to expect the daily routine of the school and had in fact become very distressed when it was interrupted by the vacation.

Initially the staff concentrated on eliminating Tommy's disruptive behaviors. When he threw a tantrum, the staff was careful to ignore him. If the tantrum persisted, or if it was interrupting a group lesson, Tommy was placed in the time-out room for 10 minutes or until his tantrum ended. During the next few weeks Tommy's tantrums became less and less frequent, and by the first vacation break they had virtually ceased. Tommy's parents were also instructed to use this extinction procedure in the hopes that the gains made at school would not be lost over the vacation.

The staff employed a behavioral shaping technique to control Tommy's hand flapping and uncontrolled running. When Tommy first began these actions, he was physically restrained by a staff member. Usually he would resist this restraint by squirming or shouting. If he started to calm down, however, he was given a reward. Effective reinforcements for him were apple slices, peanuts, and fruit juice. After several incidents Tommy learned to calm down merely in response to the staff's commands and requests. Now he was reinforced for stopping his disruptive behavior only if he did not need to be restrained. Later, as Tommy learned to remain quiet after calming down, his reinforcement became contingent on remaining in control for a set period of time, first 10 minutes, then 15, then 30, and so on. Tommy was gradually shifted from primary reinforcers (snacks) to secondary reinforcers such as hugs and praise. After six months, Tommy's hand flapping and uncontrolled running was reduced to its present level. Although he still performs these disruptive actions on occasion, he does so much less frequently than he used to, and he usually stops this behavior after a short warning from a staff member.

The next focus of therapy was to increase Tommy's level of social interaction. By selectively reinforcing his cooperative play and recreation behaviors, the staff gradually got Tommy to participate with them and with the other students in group recreation projects and unstructured play activities. Tommy's change was very slow, and even after two years he still gives little indication of empathy or interpersonal concern.

The overriding goal of Tommy's speech therapy is to increase his vocabulary. After more than two years of intensive individual and group therapy, Tommy's vocabulary has increased from 2 words to slightly over 100. Throughout the first year, Tommy refused to make any attempt at verbal communication. As a result, most of his speech training consisted of teaching him the ASL sign for various objects and concepts in his world (e.g., "teacher," "hungry," "outside"). During the training sessions, Tommy was asked to make various signs demonstrated by the speech therapist or shown on cue cards, and he was given primary reinforcers for doing so. During his second year, Tommy began to verbalize the words he was learning. As was the case with his other training, Tommy was selectively reinforced for making closer and closer approximations to the words' actual sounds. Although his articulation is very poor and the majority of his speech is incomprehensible to most people, his willingness to verbalize at least some of his thoughts represents a great advancement in his communication skills.

During summer camp Tommy's training concentrated on more basic life skills, particularly his eating behavior and his personal hygiene. By using his dessert or favorite foods as rewards, Tommy was taught to eat with utensils and to keep the majority of his food on his tray. After two weeks of having his eating carefully monitored, Tommy by and large stopped throwing food and began to use a spoon; after a month he began to use a fork, albeit sporadically. His eating habits were not otherwise affected by his camp experiences.

Another aspect of Tommy's disorder was his need to have order, predictability, and routine in his everyday life. For example, part of Tommy's hygiene training took place in the shower, where he was taught to wash himself thoroughly. It soon became clear that Tommy had a set ritual when he washed himself: left foot first, then left leg, then left side, then left arm, and so on. If he performed this washing ritual out of sequence or forgot a step, he would become very upset and would insist on repeating the entire ritual. It was not uncommon for Tommy to spend over two hours in the shower, with the counselor standing with him in the shower the entire time. In an attempt to get Tommy to give up this ritual, the counselors scheduled his showers directly before his most preferred activities, swimming and hiking. Although his showers became somewhat shorter, his shower ritual did not change significantly. On several occasions he forsook his favorite activities. Tommy's second summer as a camper also had little effect on his shower ritual. Apparently, it was more important for Tommy to complete his ritualistic behavior than to participate in his favorite recreation events.

Isolated but widely publicized cases have reported idiot savants (literally "foolish geniuses"), autistics who possess some extraordinarily well-developed ability, usually in the area of mathematical calculation or the manipulation of spatial forms. For example, Dustin Hoffman won an Oscar by portraying an idiot savant in the popular film *Rainman*. Such cases do occur in real life (see Sacks, 1985).   Daniel, a 16-year-old student at Tommy's school, could mentally add, subtract, multiply, and even divide 10-digit numbers. He also knew virtually every statistic available for every player who was ever a member of the Green Bay Packers (round drafted into the pros; number of tackles; rushing, receiving, and passing yardage). Two aspects of this phenomenon deserve mention. First, idiot savants make up but a tiny fraction all autistic cases. Second, the abilities of these autistics is usually limited to a narrow range of talents that are rarely of any practical use. For example, despite Daniel's impressive abilities at mental arithmetic, he could not make change for a dollar. Ironically the unique abilities of idiot savants might emphasize the differences between them and most other children and thus can exacerbate their social isolation.

PROGNOSIS

After more than two years at the school (including two summer camp sessions), Tommy has made limited improvement. His vocabulary has increased to over 100 words, and he is beginning to develop his speech skills. Tommy is also capable of performing some simple addition problems. For the most part, though, the progress in his communication and academic skills has been very slow, and his IQ has not changed significantly. Tommy's most noticeable change is a reduction in his disruptive behaviors. The amount of time he spends flapping his hand and running around wildly has been greatly reduced. In general, he is calmer in most situations and much easier to control. In addition, he is more cooperative during games and when working on recreation projects. Still, the staff and Tommy's parents get the impression that his cooperation is merely in response to their reinforcements; he doesn't seem to be particularly interested in pleasing others or even forming relationships with others. Tommy still spends the majority of his free time absently playing with his favorite toys, staring at his hand, or just rocking quietly. The overall prognosis for Tommy is poor. It is unlikely that he will ever be able to establish anything resembling a normal interpersonal relationship, nor will he be able to live with any degree of independence.

This discouraging prognosis is true for most children with autistic disorder. Some of the less disturbed children may eventually be able to live relatively independently in a supervised apartment or halfway house, and they may even hold down steady jobs in a sheltered work environment. A rare few will recover completely. A rough, though fairly reliable, indicator of a child's prognosis is his or her attainment of speech skills. By and large, children who have developed recognizable speech by the age of 5 will be able to benefit most from therapy and have the greatest chance of eventually living on their own. Most of the more severely disturbed children, however, will probably require professional care for the rest of their lives.

Finally, it is important to note that the behaviors of autistic children, both their disruptive actions and their persistent rejection of social attachments, are very taxing for the people who must deal with them on a regular basis. At Tommy's school the staff often joked that the eight-hour school days, and especially the eight-week summer camp, were more therapeutic for the parents than for the students, and in all likelihood this was true. Treating autistic children is a grueling process with few rewards, and many professionals lose motivation in the face of the slow progress of their students. During Tommy's first two years at the school, two full-time staff members quit, and there was constant turnover in the student volunteer program. The summer camp counselors were especially prone to burnout. Of the twelve camp counselors who worked with Tommy (all psychology and special education majors from several different colleges), not one returned for a second year, and only one decided to pursue a career in mental health! But the option of quitting is not available to parents of autistic children, whose only choice is to persevere or to institutionalize their child. This is a bleak prognosis, indeed.

SELECTED REFERENCES

Alcoholics Anonymous. (1976). (3rd. ed.). New York: Alcoholics Anonymous World Services, Inc.

American Psychiatric Association. (2000). *Diagnostic and statistical manual of mental disorders* (4th ed. text rev). Washington, DC: Author.

Andreasen, N. C., & Olsen, S. A. (1982). Negative versus positive schizophrenia: Definition and validation. *Archives of General Psychiatry, 39*, 789–794.

Burns, D. (1980/1999). *Feeling good: The new mood therapy.* New York: HarperCollins Publishers.

Carpenter, K. (1972). *I won't last a day without you.* Los Angeles: A&M.

Cermak, T. L. (1986). *Diagnosing and treating adult children of alcoholics.* Minneapolis: Johnson Institute Books.

Cermak, T. L., & Brown, S. (1982). Interactional group therapy with adult children of alcoholics. *International Journal of Group Psychotherapy, 32,* 375–389.

Conners, C. K., Erhardt, D., & Sparrow, E. (1999). *Conner's Adult ADHD Rating Scales (CAARS), technical manual.* New York: Multi-Health Systems.

Cullen, M., & Freeman-Longo, R. E. (1996). *Men & anger.* Holyoke, MA: NEARI Press.

Goodman, W. K., Price, L. H., Rasmussen, S. A., Mazure, C., Fleischmann, R. L., Hill, C. H., Heninger, G. R., & Charney, D. S. (1989). *The Yale-Brown Obsessive-Compulsive Scale: I. Development, use, and reliability. Archives of General Psychiatry, 46,* 1006–1011.

Goodman, W. K., Price, L. H., Rasmussen, S. A., Mazure, C., Delgado, P., Heninger, G. R., & Charney, D. S. (1989). *The Yale-Brown Obsessive-Compulsive Scale: II. Validity. Archives of General Psychiatry, 46,* 1012–1016.

Hallowell, E. M., & Ratey, J. (1994). *Driven to distraction: Recognizing and coping with attention deficit disorder from childhood through adulthood.* New York: Pantheon Press.

Hauri, P. J. (1991). Case studies in insomnia. New York: Plenum Press.

Kanner, L. (1943). Autistic disturbances of effective content. *Nervous Child, 2,* 217–240.

Kaplan, H. S. (1974). *The new sex therapy.* New York: Brunner/Mazel.

Klerman, G. L., Weissman, M. M., Rounsaville, B. J., & Chevron, S. E. (1984). *Interpersonal psychotherapy of depression.* New York: Basic Books.

Kluft, R. P. (1984). Aspects of the treatment of multiple personality disorder. *Psychiatric Annals, 14,* 51–55.

Kroll, J. (1988). *The challenge of the borderline patient: Competency in diagnosis and treatment.* New York: Norton.

Kushner, H. (1981/2001). *When bad things happen to good people.* New York: Schocken Books.

Linehan, M. M. (1993). *Cognitive-behavioral treatment of borderline personality disorder: The dialectics of effective treatment.* New York: Guilford.

Masters, W., & Johnson, V. (1970). *Human sexual inadequacy.* Boston: Little, Brown.

Rasmussen, S. A., & Eisen, J. L. (1989). Clinical features and phenomenology of obsessive-compulsive disorder. *Psychiatric Annals, 19,* 67–73.

Regier, D. A., Boyd, J. H., Burke, J. D., Rae, D. S., Myers, J. K., Kramer, M., Robins, L. N., George, L. K., Karno, M., & Locke, B. Z. (1988). One-month prevalence of mental disorders in the United States: Based on five epidemiologic catchment area sites. *Archives of General Psychiatry, 45,* 977–986.

Ross, C. A. (1997). *Dissociative identity disorder: Diagnosis, clinical features, and treatment of multiple personality* (2nd ed.). New York: Wiley.

References

Sacks, O. (1985). *The man who mistook his wife for a hat, and other clinical tales.* New York: Summit Books.

Shapiro, F. (1995). *Eye movement desensitization and reprocessing: Basic principles, protocols and procedures* (1st ed.). New York: Guilford Press.

Shapiro, F. (2002). EMDR twelve years after its introduction: A review of past, present, and future directions. *Journal of Clinical Psychology, 58,* 1–22.

Spiegel, D. (1996). Dissociative disorders. In R. E. Hales & S. C. Yudofsky (Eds.), *The American Psychiatric Press synopsis of psychiatry* (pp. 583–604). Washington, D.C.: American Psychiatric Press.

Wechsler, D. (1991). *Manual for the Wechsler Preschool and Primary Intelligence Scale* (3rd ed.). San Antonio: Psychological Corporation.